Citizen of the World

Soon-Young and the UN

Citizen of the World

Soon-Young and the UN

Soon-Young Yoon

Ewha Womans University Press

Citizen of the World

Soon-Young and the UN

Written By Soon-Young Yoon

First published 3 August 2021
by Ewha Womans University Press
52, Ewhayeodae-gil, Seodaemun-gu, Seoul, Korea, 03760
Tel. : 82-2-3277-2965, 362-6076
Fax. : 82-2-312-4312
E-mail: press@ewha.ac.kr

ISBN 979-11-5890-434-0 03330
Price: 28,000 won

Contents

Chapter 3 • Violence against Women

Chapter 4 • Finding the Earth's Balance

Chapter 5 • Claiming the Right to Health

Chapter 6 • Economic Empowerment

Chapter 7 • Collective Voices

Chapter 8 • Circle of Women: Portraits

Preface

I am hardly an expert on how the United Nations works, but I am happy to share with you what I have learned from personal experience. As an anthropologist, I have worked inside and outside the UN. I have traveled to every region of the world to discuss global problems with some of the world's most interesting people, including villagers, traditional healers, scholars, UN officials, and heads of state.

Through the years, I have succeeded in making the UN an intimate part of my identity. Like a cannibal hoping to capture their powerful spirits, I have devoured UN documents in bits and pieces. I can assure you that UN documents are—pardon the expression—excellent food for thought. What about all that jargon? Once you enjoy the excellent flavor of the ideas, the hard-to-understand stuff is just gristle around the edges.

You might ask, "Why bother trying to understand the UN?" Millions of people think that the UN isn't delivering on its promises. However, I have seen the UN bottom-up from the vantage point of refugees, lepers, survivors of sexual violence, rural girls, and indigenous peoples. For them, ideas at the UN bring hope and promise for a better world. The UN represents what governments once aspired to for all of humanity: human rights, equality, development, and peace.

What is the UN's future? Through the years, I have learned one truth: the UN will be what we make of it. The secret is for all of us to take responsibility for its progress.

This is an excellent era to be involved with the UN. 2012 marked Korea's Year of the Water Dragon, the launch of a new cosmic cycle of 60 years. We are living in the dragon's time when courage, creativity and imagination will be rewarded. Let us imagine a new and better beginning.

S Yoon

Acknowledgments

I was very excited when Pranay Gupte, publisher and editor of *The Earth Times*, called and suggested that I write columns for the newspaper. Many of my writings that appeared between 1996 and 2000 are the inspiration for the content of this book. Tanya Selvaratnam offered her creative advice that covers many subjects. Galin Dechoian and Soyeon Kim added their grammatical touch. I thank Richard M. Smith, my linguistic consultant and love of my life, who helps to expand my evolving universe of the English lexicon.

Chapter 1

About me

Why I Joined the UN

My friends sometimes ask why I chose to work at the United Nations rather than in academia. The answer is simple. Universities may be a good vantage point to watch social change, but the UN is a better place to make a global impact. The leap from academia to the UN was an adventurous leap that has provided endless lessons about the world's cultures and how the UN affects the everyday lives of the poor and forgotten. My work as a former social development officer for UNICEF often involved listening to people's experiences with the UN, evaluating project impacts, and making recommendations for improvements.

Rural women taught me important lessons about how development projects often get things wrong. For example, information campaigns about women's sexual and reproductive health sometimes missed the mark. In one village, women told me that they didn't need any more information about family planning. The truth was they couldn't use it anyways because their husbands would beat them if they even mentioned using contraceptives.

At other times, the UN was in the right place doing exactly what

A WHO meeting (1983)

was needed. Women shared good news of how UNICEF helped them develop income generation projects and how more money in their pockets empowered them to end harmful practices like female genital mutilation. I visited orphanages for the deaf where UNICEF worked hand-in-hand with NGOs to train children how to speak. There were water and sanitation projects saving lives because children could wash their hands in clean water. This wasn't the highest form of diplomacy—no polished speeches here. This was the United Nations in action.

Several years later, I worked as a social scientist at the World Health Organization's Southeast Asia Regional Office (SEARO). When I learned that I was being considered for the job again, I jumped at the chance because of its intensive, hands-on course in public health. At the time, I was the only social scientist at a WHO Regional Office working with WHO's Geneva headquarters. Numerous social science programs were being added to the social science and health programs, such as child immunization, AIDS, tropical diseases, reproductive health and environmental health. I had a crash course in all of these subjects. Through field visits, I saw the plight of the disenfranchised who suffered while waiting for the UN and governments to take action.

What do I think are the most important qualities of someone who applies for a job at the UN?

I would put courage and compassion at the top of the list. You have to be willing to go to dangerous places. Compassion for human suffering is equally important. There is nothing more discrediting to the UN than an officer who doesn't show kindness to the people they serve.

I admit that some parts of the UN are handicapped by a culture of bureaucracy around following rules. Call me a romantic, but I believe that the UN survives because it is a bureaucracy. The best UN bureaucrats do the job they were assigned, whether advising governments on the best way to eradicate malaria or arranging microphones for a meeting. I also think that the organization is what we make of it. Take the same "worthless" job and fill it with a motivated, qualified activist. You have a completely different result. The UN is only as strong and effective as the governments that we put in place to govern it.

Even with these vestiges of a bureaucratic morass, the UN remains the most universal and fair-handed champion of the underdogs, the forgotten, and the underserved. Rich and powerful nations are forced to listen to the smallest country, and enemies find neutral territory on which to face off—and head off—deadly conflicts. It's the most democratic institution I know. Every country, regardless of its size and power, has one vote.

Today, the UN is facing a great challenge as governments try to dismantle multilateralism and discredit notions of global citizenship. Yet, I am confident that the UN can survive if it looks for and nurtures innovation. Some creative ideas can come from within, but most will come from the social movements surrounding the UN. The connection between social movements and the UN was at the founding of the UN and must stay strong. They have the vision and dedication to causes like gender equality, environmental justice, and racial equality.

The Koreans Are Coming

In the late 1970s, South Korea's economic miracle was in full swing. President Park Chung-Hee had a leadership style reminiscent of Japanese colonial rule. Many of my friends were arrested and tortured by the Korean Central Intelligence Agency (KCIA). Labor union leaders and protestors disappeared without a trace. The Christian-inspired urban labor movement was in turmoil, its human rights principles entirely at odds with the dictatorship. Throughout this period, student protests and proclamations for the freedom of imprisoned poets, scholars, and journalists led to clashes with the police.

The women's studies program at Ewha Womans University and its leadership training center for women rural leaders quickly attracted the attention of Korean intelligence agents. Faculty members involved were routinely harassed. What bothered the KCIA officers the most was not the idea of women's liberation; it was the notion that women wanted to be the ones to make decisions about who and what was involved in Korea's future.

The international press also played an important role in reporting on Korea's progress. I met Rick Smith, an editor for *Newsweek* maga-

• *Newsweek* cover story (1977)

zine who wanted to learn more about the labor movement. He was a tall—very tall—and lanky young man who intimidated most Koreans in an elevator. I sometimes described him as my biological opposite with his Irish-American blond hair and fair eyes. When we walked down a busy street, both facing forward, he often complained he couldn't hear what I was saying and vice versa. I think I grew several inches from just stretching my neck to send my voice upwards.

My research projects had put me in touch with the mother of Chun Tae-Il, a revered figure in the textile labor movement who made international headlines when he immolated himself in protest against the Park dictatorship. Rick Smith wanted to interview her and hear

• Our wedding photo

the other side of the story on Korea's economic miracle. I made sure he got his story. These were the days when the government hired people to cut out censored passages of international magazines. Of course, the moment we saw the missing parts, everyone immediately sought out clandestine copies of the article. Impressed by the power of reporting the truth to the outside world, I began to take greater interest in journalists—and in him.

Rick and I were soon traveling around the country together, making both of us even more suspect to the KCIA. Intelligence agents hovered around the school residence hall, asking whether I was breaking the National Security Act by giving anti-government information to the foreign press. Agents were also obsessed with another question: were Rick and I married? That may seem to be an odd query by American standards, but in Korean culture, marriage information is considered basic data on par with one's age and sex. I imagined that our files were being misplaced as one agent put us with the "married couples" files while another would separate our papers. There were other aspects of their inquiries that were less amusing.

When Rick Smith's cover story for "The Koreans Are Coming" issue of *Newsweek* finally reached the stands, it added fuel to the controversy around the contrast between the growing Korean economy and a hardline dictatorship. Needless to say, it was the first of many stories he would write about Korea. He continued to ask me for interviews, and I was pleased to be quoted occasionally in *Newsweek*. Although we were born in different worlds, this meeting in Korea was to set us on a life journey together. We were eventually married by nine Buddhist monks in Thailand. In 2021, we celebrated our 43rd wedding anniversary.

Education: Our Family's Security Blanket

My maternal grandfather, Song Sang-Chum, was an unusually tall man of over 6 feet tall. His hair was cut short in a similar style of school boys, and he often dressed in white Korean traditional clothing. He was known as one of the most innovative modern leaders in Pyongyang at the time.

An ardent advocate of social equality, he wanted his family to dedicate themselves to Korea's modernization in an effort to protect Korea from foreign powers. At the turn of the 20th century, Pyongyang was the industrial center of the country and under Japanese occupation. However, when compared to the West, it lacked modernized agriculture or a strong manufacturing sector.

My grandfather's problem was that he had only one son and many daughters, so he raised his independent, assertive daughters to join his "development corps." He told his friends that his girls could beat any boy at almost anything. He was determined to educate them abroad, so they could bring back the best of foreign ideas. He wanted each child to learn different skills in Western medicine, the arts, agriculture, and education. He also believed that Japanese military rule

• Song Sang-Chum

could be overthrown if Korea could have a strong economy.

The first child to study abroad was my mother's sister, Song Pok-Shyn. A slight person with a fragile physique and nerves of steel, she went to a missionary high school for girls in Pyongyang and was excited about opportunities abroad. My grandfather wanted her to study modern medicine, so even before she went to medical school in Japan, he built a Western-style hospital in Pyongyang.

His plans went astray when my rebellious aunt joined the anti-Japanese underground. She worked as a secret courier, carrying messages for the provisional government in Manchuria. My aunt was eventually arrested, imprisoned, and tortured for her anti-colonial activities. She fled to the United States and was told to never return. Through sheer determination, she received a Barbour Scholarship at Universi-

My mother's house in Pyungyang

ty of Michigan. She became the first Korean woman in the United States to earn a PhD in public health in 1929. For the rest of her life in the United States, she continued to open doors for women's equality.

My aunt was a great help to my mother, Song Kyung-Shyn, who was a soft-spoken, artistic spirit who charmed everyone with her playful wit. When my mother was a little girl, she dreamed of studying piano in the United States. She had already toured China with the Pyongyang Symphony Orchestra at the age of ten without my grandfather. What still amazes me is that he even accompanied her to late night rehearsals on the outskirts of the city. He bought her a German piano and agreed that she could go abroad to study. At age 16, she entered the American Conservatory of Music. When she finished school, she returned to Pyongyang and married Yoon Doo-Sun, my father and a musician. They achieved their dream of establishing the first Western-style music conservatory in North Korea.

However, times were troubled, and our family's future was threatened. The Russian army seized our house and turned it into its headquarters. It was time to leave. Eventually, the entire family made its way hundreds of miles from Pyongyang to Seoul. Within a few months, we were heading to a new home and a peaceful life in the

United States.

Through my aunt's diplomatic ties in Washington, D.C., she arranged for a U.S. military ship to give us safe passage from Busan to San Francisco. John A. Hannah, the former head of USAID and then-president of Michigan State University, invited my parents to teach music. Thus, my parents re-established their lives in Michigan. They could rebuild their lives from nothing because they had carried with them a treasure that no one could take away: their education.

• Song Kyung-Shyn in America

Interview: Escape from Pyongyang

Why did you leave your hometown of Pyongyang?

I left Pyongyang in 1947. Pyongyang was under Russian military authority at the time. Life for my family had not been easy and was about to get worse. During the Japanese occupation, my good-natured mother, Song Kyung-Shyn, surrendered her brass housewares and even her wedding ring to the Japanese army, who supposedly needed more metal for arms. When the Russians and Chinese militaries arrived, my parents' music school was shut down, and the rest of the family properties had to be handed over to the armies. My rebellious father refused to join the communist army. When we learned that soldiers were coming to arrest him, my parents decided that it was time to escape to the south.

What do you remember about leaving?

I was awakened in the middle of the night and told that we were going on a long journey. I could not take any of my toys, and I would have to be very quiet. I had no idea that my family planned to escape from

• First family portrait in America (1947)

Communist rule. Between us and Seoul, there was a desolate, heavily armed frontier. In that no-man's land, Russians were known to shoot anything that moved. Nevertheless, there were secret networks of paid workers who helped refugees to cross the 38th parallel. My parents planned to use that clandestine network to get the family to safety in Seoul. We were left with my grandmother in a remote settlement outside Pyongyang. I did not know where my parents had gone for three months.

As a child, I hardly understood the meaning of the 38th parallel, but it seemed so important to my parents. I thought that it traversed the entire world and that everyone lived on one side or the other. I wondered, 'Why the number 38? Were there 38 soldiers guarding it? Was it made of 38 walls? And how did I ever get from one side to the other?' I understood crossing a river or a room but not a national border.

Many refugees from North Korea left empty-handed. How did your family survive?

My father, Yoon Doo-Sun, had a good sense for business. Back then, milled wood was like currency and more valuable than gold in the south, where there was an acute housing shortage. My father left on a motorboat with his lumber and traveled south by night along the coast. When he arrived in Seoul, he presented a letter of introduction to a friend who worked with the border authorities, thinking that it would serve as legitimate identification. Instead of giving him refuge, his friend confiscated his lumber, accused him of being a spy, and threw him into Seoul's Namsan Prison.

What about your mother?

My mother stayed behind because she was about to give birth. She learned of my father's imprisonment through a network of women traders who crossed the 38th parallel to sell gold. After giving birth to a stillborn baby, she was determined to go to Seoul alone to free my father. Her cousin, Park Ke-Ung, was an influential businessman in Seoul and would be able to help.

I can hardly imagine the courage it took for her to leave home. Because she was too weak to walk, she hired a rowboat owned by a family who lived near the border. They hid her under the boat's planks, where she lay all night. Just before dawn, she walked onto the shore south of the border. She carried one small bag of possessions from her past life into the new.

How did you travel?

My mother's loyal sister, Song Do-Shyn, traveled back across the 38th parallel from South Korea to fetch me and my siblings. For the first part of the journey, my family was able to hire a truck. Then the older children had to walk, and my aunt carried me on her back. My four-year-old sister, Kyung-Cha, and older brothers, Duk-Yung and Duk-

Yong, walked for almost two days and nights. When we got to the 38th parallel, men were hired to carry the children across the border. This part of the journey had to be completed in the dark. Russian soldiers spotted us on our first try and chased us back to the north. We set out again by a different route. When we finally made it to Seoul, we had lost a lot of weight.

During our travels, I became very ill and ran a high fever. Uncertain that I would ever see my parents again, I would wake up from nightmares. The recurrent dream that I had for many years was about refugees crossing an icy river at night. The currents were strong, and chunks of broken ice bobbed in the black waters. The bridges had been blown up, so everyone had to cross by foot. In my dreams, I saw a woman who drowned when pulled down through the ice by the weight of the baby on her back. I doubt that I ever saw such events in real life. The dreams were much more frightening because I became the baby in the dream.

How do you think this childhood experience influenced you?

Growing up, I always felt that global events can affect your daily life. Wars, climate change, terrorism, and financial crises can turn your world upside down and take away everything you love. I have also always assumed that politics could go in the wrong direction at any time. The sense of insecurity can have positive effects because it inspires you to act instead of assuming someone else will work it out for you. It also prepares you to accept sudden disasters, act quickly, and overcome fears.

Chapter 2

Navigating the Boundaries of Identities

"If every path you take comes back to you,
then you will never move ahead."
_ Kung Fu Panda

Introduction

I never thought that potatoes and onions would ever attract my intellectual curiosity, but lately, these two legumes have turned into a giant metaphor about gender and politics. Potatoes as a cornerstone of political analysis appeared long ago when Karl Marx wrote about French peasants as potatoes in a sack. Marx didn't think highly of the French landed peasantry as an ingredient in his recipe for class revolt. If anything, this highly individualistic, entrepreneurial group symbolized everything he didn't like: citizens who would never unite as a class to defend their own interests. He turned his attention instead to the industrial working class. He hailed factory workers and their potential for direct action with flattering metaphors, none of which were vegetables.

A gender perspective on Marx' metaphor about potatoes and peasants exposes a gender bias in his assumptions. As feminist scholars have often noted, he had only one gender in mind: men. Taking his analysis one step further, we can raise the unflattering analogy to an outright insult. The exterior of the potato holds its main nutrients, seeds, and cellular complexity. On the other hand, the innards are dismissed as uniformly bland. Drenched in gravies, curries, sugar, and spices, their true flavors are hidden. As the ultimate culinary chameleon, the potato's essence is kept hidden from view.

My latest thought about women is that we are not potatoes but rather a flavorful collection of onions. The complexities of private life are much more exposed for women. Each of us carries around layer upon layer of identities.

Being a woman is just one way I see myself as an onion. Peeling away other identities to arrive at this is not only possible, but it can be done without crying. In fact, for many women who join in a demonstration or successfully rally around International Women's Day, the creation of a oneness that is united across all differences is an empowering experience.

The world's women and girls have become more than vegetables thrown together into a sack. We have peeled away layers of our many identities until we found a common identity. Our consciousness as women is almost primitive, primordial, and fundamental enough to let us join hands with strangers from different nationalities and to pledge allegiance to each other's causes. Whether we are English, Mohican, Zambian, or Burmese, we manage to find a common bond at our core as wives, mothers, sisters and women. We often rally around each other's issues with one voice, no matter the various issues we hold most dear.

It feels good to be an onion. It feels even better to know that you are in the company of others—in fact, a little more than half of the world's population. I credit feminists for forging this mass sisterhood. We picked an identity that is one of the biggest categories of the human species. Maybe the more we have, the more we know that we are still growing. I wish that men could cross over the gender line, so they could understand how much fun it can be to be female.[1]

---

1 For an elaboration of this idea, read the article on "How to Peel an Onion without Crying."

Mothers and Sons

Did you ever hear the riddle about the boy whose father was a famous surgeon? The child grew up fine and strong, but when he was 15-years-old, he and his father got into a car accident. By chance, they were taken to different hospitals. The boy's critical condition required immediate treatment. The emergency surgeon said, "I can't operate on him. He's my son." (Hospital rules prohibited physicians from operating on members of their own family.) The mystery is: who was the doctor?

Give up? The surgeon was his mother, so she could not treat her child. If you took more than ten seconds to answer the riddle, you probably should admit that you're struggling with gender stereotypes. Don't worry. Women do not typically think of surgeons as female either. In most countries, they're not. High-level medical specialists, hospital administrators, and ministers of health are male on the average. On the other hand, nurses, lab technicians, and medical secretaries are mostly women. This gender hierarchy in healthcare reflects a general trend in the sciences, such as engineering, environmental sciences, physics, and mathematics. The same holds true in the multibil-

• Dr. Suh Kwang-Sun and President Kim Hae-Sook at Ewha (2018)

lion-dollar health industry, where women work mostly in the lower paying jobs.

The UN Commission on the Status of Women recommends that governments take stronger measures to end the gender gap in science and technology education. However, this will take considerable effort because it takes centuries to undo male biases. For example, Britain's elite Royal Society did not admit women until 1945. Unequal access to education, cultural biases against science and technology careers for girls, and other lifelong limitations have contributed to fewer women at the top of their scientific fields. By 2020, only 23 women have been awarded Nobel Prizes in the sciences and medicine compared to 599 men.

We have to learn more about how education can make a difference in countries with staunch patriarchal traditions. Universities like

Ewha Womans University in Seoul, Korea, (the largest women's university in the world with 25,000 students) have made great advances in breaking gender stereotypes. Male administrators like Dr. Suh Kwang-Sun, former Dean of the Graduate school, were pioneers launching women's studies and encouraging other male faculty to challenge Confucian educational norms. Within a few decades this university helped nurture a generation of women health leaders, medical scientists, and feminist doctors.

We hardly know enough about this process cross-culturally. It would be fascinating to conduct an anthropological study of sons with mothers who are professionals in medicine and the sciences. Do these boys adjust well to the idea that a woman can compete in a man's world? When these sons grow up, are they more likely to be supportive husbands of working wives? Do they become better teachers and encourage female students to pursue any career they want? My intuitive response is an optimistic yes.

In addition to the influence of UN and government policies, changes in men's attitudes can make a difference. In Sweden, the women's movement has inspired a men's movement for gender equality—an interesting trend that merits more attention. Women who have achieved recognition in the sciences and technology can also influence a generation of young men to give gender equality a chance. Boys need women as role models too.

Competing on a Level Playing Field

When my daughter was 12-years-old, she came home proudly holding broken blocks of wood. She held them like prize plaques, one in each hand.

"Guess what? I broke this with my foot today at Taekwondo class," she said.

I stared in amazement at the one-inch-thick pieces with their stone-like surfaces. She swore that it was easy if you hit the block fast and hard enough. At my request, she demonstrated the martial arts motions. She clenched her fists as the right side of her torso swiftly twisted upward. Her knee locked, then released with an aggressive snap into the air. Only the blood-curdling cry of triumph was missing. I moved aside to give her more room to repeat the kick.

Judged by traditional Korean standards, her body movements could hardly be called "feminine." Conventional social rules dictate that female gestures should be close to the body—inward and folded, not splitting apart in the air. A hand should cover the mouth when laughing. The knees should be together when sitting. These conventions of poise and modesty become part of a corporal repertoire that

• Our daughter learns Taekwondo

the body learns from early childhood.

Playing sports helps the body widen its range of personal expressions and identities. There are more good reasons to support public sports programs for girls. When girls are allowed to compete equally with boys in sports, their self-esteem seems to gain ground. Fathers should not hesitate to make sure their daughters' confidence increases. In the 1920s, my mother caused a scandal in high school by playing sports in Pyongyang. Her long Korean skirt got a little in the way, but she chased a ball around the courts with the boys. Swimming in the river was also on her list of after-school activities. Her confidence to pursue these interests got a boost when my grandfather publicly supported her "tomboy" behavior.

I'm not suggesting that girls should fight their way through a hockey match or take up violent sports just to prove their worth. Emulating these "masculine" behaviors are low on my list of what sports should teach girls. However, sports teach invaluable life skills and lessons, like team playing, leadership and discipline. Sports can help girls feel more secure about their bodies, because they are evaluated on how they perform, not how they look.

Courage is another character trait that a challenging physical activity can contribute to positive self-image to girls. Many children who study Taekwondo can't strike the wood (or a brick) forcefully enough because of a natural childlike fear of self-inflicted injury. As my daughter overcame her apprehension, she pushed herself into the unknown. She took an important step forward to improving her self-esteem. That gave her a high score in my books for sportsmanship.

We should add ten points for what really counts: she bet her right foot on the possibility that she could succeed. That show of courage is the real reason I installed her broken pieces of wood in the family Hall of Fame on a high shelf for all to admire. It reminds us of that one glorious day when she hit a target just right, breaking a block of wood and opening a space that would always be hers.

The Big Bindi Controversy

During a meeting at the Asia Institute for Science and Technology in Bangkok, Thailand, I approached a student to ask about Canada's foreign assistance in South Asia. However, the topic of conversation quickly changed when I couldn't take my eyes off the black plastic dot that decorated her forehead. Known as the bindi, the dot is a common accessory for young Indian women. In this case, its large size almost overwhelmed the symmetry of her eyes.

"That sure is a big bindi," I said. She laughed and lifted her eyebrows to animate the bindi into a playful wiggle. Everyone has a distinguishing trademark, and this was hers.

"I'm known for my big bindis," she explained.

I asked her opinion about the origin of the bindi. "For most modern Indian women, it is just a decoration like a nose ring or bangles," she said when I asked for her opinion on the origin of the bindi. "I suspect men invented it to distract other men's attention away from their wives' beautiful eyes. For me, a bindi is a decoy. It's the first thing that strangers see before our eyes meet. It gives me a chance to give them a quick look-over."

I wear a bindi and Indian dress (1985)

The foreign aid debate was put aside. The origin of the bindi had to be settled. A small group gathered around to listen to my theory. I had heard that the bindi originated in religious rituals. After prayers, Hindu priests always bless male and female devotees with red powder called the tika. Some scholars say that the tika is a religious symbol representing a drop of blood of demons killed by the goddess Durga, a marker of victory of good over evil. Now that's the kind of cosmic power everyone should be proud to carry around on their heads.

What about the bindi from a feminist perspective? According to custom in rural India, only married women have the right to wear it. Young girls are not allowed to do so, and widows must give up their bindis. The discussion was rapidly turning into a feminist critique of the bindi. We questioned why widows didn't have the right to adorn their heads any way they wish. One observer pointed out that maybe widows were happy to be free from the mark.

"I think the bindi was originally used to mark slaves," said a student, "and married women in India are slaves to their husbands." That remark promoted a lot of muttering in the affirmative, and it looked for a moment as if these students were going to take to the streets in a mass revolt.

Cooler heads prevailed at the end of the day, and there were no demonstrations. Some young women noted that old taboos are changing these days. It's unclear whether the bindi symbolizes women's spiritual power, marital bondage, or maybe some kind of natural fashion sense. The bindi is obviously in the eye of the beholder. Whatever its origins, this simple plastic dot on a person's forehead is clearly full of cultural meaning and deeply embedded in issues of identity. More research needs to be done.

For now, my conclusion is simple: bindi is as bindi does—and big bindis do it better.

Hairy Tales and Rebellious Girls

If you are having a bad hair day and want to try a radical look, you might want to consider how such a dramatic makeover might be received in other cultures. In some societies, your haircut reveals your cultural and possibly even your political leanings. Our coiffures are like billboards, sending instant messages "I am willing to compromise" or "Don't you dare tell me what to do." If you revolutionize the outside of your head, you could be projecting what is going on inside.

Girls throughout the ages have changed their hairstyles as a sign of political rebellion. You would be surprised how some patriarchal authorities have reacted. Take the famous case of the students in Sichuan province during the 1920s. At the time, girls wore long braids and did not cut their hair until marriage. Qin De-jun, a believer in equal rights for women, had other ideas. She joined a progressive group called the Intuition Society and began to dress like a man. One day, she cut her hair short, and two other female students did the same. Her style, known as the Napoleon, was straight and considered very "unfeminine."

Qin's mother caused a scene because she believed that cutting hair

• Nepalese girls like long hair (1990)

before marriage revealed corrupt morals and violated Confucian teachings. The girls had to leave school. One was sent back to her hometown. Another was forced to marry against her wishes. Qin left home and joined the Students' Autonomous Association at another girls' school. Social reformers had heard about her outrageous short hair and rallied to her cause. The association even organized a play about her haircutting incident.

The Napoleon and Washington hairstyles eventually turned into a movement that swept the province. Conservative parties rallied against the students and alerted the police, saying that if the girls were allowed to continue, their rebellion would affect the morality of the state. As a result, the police issued a prohibition on short haircuts for girls. Unfortunately, for parents, placing a ban on hairstyles rarely lasts. When you walk down the streets of modern Beijing, you can easily assess which side of this controversy won.

There is a boys' side of this hairy tale as well. In most cultures, femininity is identified by long hair, so boys who let their hair grow out are believed to have crossed the gender line. In several cultures, long hair for boys is taboo. Before Princess Diana's visit to Nepal in 1993, the Nepalese police rounded up long-haired boys in the streets and shaved them into crew-cuts in an attempt to make them more "respectable." The move backfired, and the young men earned a lot of public sympathy. Newspapers carried editorials with titles like "Spare my hair" and "Long live long hair." There were also serious stories about the boys' human rights and hair rights.

If you think that making decisions about your hair are important, you're dead right. Also, if you live in a society where you—and not the police—are the ones to decide how your hair looks, be thankful, live it up, and try something new. I hear that Jell-O makes a good green.

The Nurturing Instinct

A father bends over to look at his tiny newborn daughter, and his nurturing instincts stir inside. To give her a head start on a future career as an actress, he tries to teach her his favorite folk song. He barely looks at the infant in public, but in the privacy of his home, he plays age-old baby games, like peekaboo or clicking his tongue to get a reaction. If the baby should accidentally gurgle, he declares that she recognizes him. In his eyes, she is already the most intelligent child in the world—and she is only three days old. If this baby turns out to be a genius, her father will probably deserve some credit.

We used to think that children's brains are genetically determined by the time they are born. Thanks to positron emission tomography (PET), which images the brain, it seems that nurturing activities, like rocking, singing, and talking to babies, actually stimulates the brain's development. This development can start very early in life. Apparently, babies in the womb can recognize their parents' voices. A child only four days old can tell the difference between the French "Bonjour, mon petit chou." and English "Hello, my little cabbage."

Some traditional childrearing practices in developing countries may even have unusually positive effects on brain development. For example, in most Asian, African, and Latin American cultures, there is prolonged physical interaction between parents and infants, particularly in poor households where mothers do not hire caretakers. In Latin America and Southeast Asia, many mothers carry children all day as they work. African families often sleep with children, so it is rare for a child less than three years old to be alone. From the Western point of view, this continual contact with the child might seem excessive. As one American woman said, "Doesn't the baby need a break from all that attention? Maybe a little privacy?"

Knowing this, what happens to victims of domestic violence, refugees, or street children? Scientists report that trauma inflicts irreparable damage to the brain's neurotransmitter and that stress hormones wash over the brain, contributing to the possibility of abnormal brain development. There are many questions. Does this mean that all children less than three years who have lived through wars will be intellectually disabled? What happens to those who are nutritionally deprived?

According to UNICEF, in Bangladesh, it is estimated that nearly one half of babies are born malnourished and with a low birth weight. We know that this puts them at a disadvantage for proper physiological development. However, does this also mean that these children will also have learning problems? Probably not. The truth is: we do not know. We don't have definitive answers about how cultural differences in child-rearing influence the intricate interactions between social environments and childhood brain development. Until we have answers, we must avoid falling into the facile, cultural determinist view that a disadvantaged child is a lost cause because of poverty.

Even in extreme poverty, grandfathers, fathers, older brothers, and other male family members can help mothers with child development. Men can promote healthy intellectual growth from day one. This doesn't mean that the men have to use flash cards or high-tech learning aids with their infants. It only takes the usual "goo-goo, ga-ga" fun, loving care, good nutrition, and... well... maybe more of that singing.

What Men Can Do as Feminists

At the UN, the governments of Iceland and Suriname sponsored a "barbershop" conference for male ambassadors, so they could "let down their hair" and talk confidentially about male behavior and gender identities. Greta Gunnarsdottir, Iceland's former ambassador to the UN, thought of this unconventional event because she wanted to see what role men could play in combatting violence against women and gender discrimination. I overheard one ambassador say, "The majority of men don't beat their wives, so we need to start by talking with other men about why this is happening." This speaks to the problem I've always had with women's fight to end violence against women. We are not the source of the problem, so why do we think it is our sole responsibility to fix it?

Good politicians have learned that women leaders do not like men to speak for them. However, there is a lot that men can do to speak up. Spokesmen in the male-dominated arenas of politics, economics, and cultural and social life can and should take a more active role in reforming men's attitudes about girls and women. Groups like Man Up and the White Ribbon Campaign are setting excellent examples

• The barbershop conference with Greta Gunnarsdottir and Phumzile Mlambo Ngcuka to her left (2015)

of how men can validate and support the women's movement by taking the lead in reforming themselves.

Men can also contribute to gender equality by re-examining their roles as husbands, fathers, and sons. In the biographies of many outstanding women leaders, including my revolutionary aunt, there is an approving and encouraging father, uncle, grandfather, or teacher. When it comes to decisions on inheritance, marriage, or education, a father's strong stand on equal financial help for girls in the family can turn the tide of a family quarrel.

It should go without saying that all men should loudly condemn both the practice and practitioners of spousal or child abuse. Sons and brothers can be particularly effective allies of girls in their families. Men should be encouraged to join in the UN's battle against domestic violence through awareness training and human rights education for boys. And this should start at the highest levels of the UN and in governments because men's leadership for gender justice matters.

The next generation is changing. More young men are sympathetic to—and even calling themselves—feminists. Young men and non-binary people who become involved in the women's movement are markedly more courageous than men of the older generation. Some are enjoying the new experience. One young Arab man volunteered to photocopy documents for me during a meeting of women's organizations in Amman, Jordan. When I asked him how he came to help at a women's meeting, he laughed and said, "Look, when I told my friends I was going to help at a meeting with 1,200 women, they all asked where they could sign up."

These men would be interested in the definition of gender. Gender is the social relations between men and women and patterns of behavior which are cultural, not biological. If unequal treatment for women is learned behavior, it can also change. This gender concept can work to men's advantage as well. Some women are coming around to the idea that men are not destined to be male chauvinist pigs by nature. Now, isn't that a reason to take heart?

Racism Is Thin Skinned

They say that you have to educate children about racism, but kids can sometimes teach a good lesson to grown-ups. When my daughter, Song-Mee, was four years old, she asked me how to tell who was Korean and who was not. Trying to keep it simple, I told her that most Koreans had black hair.

A few days later, my Ethiopian friend, Belkis, visited. Song-Mee came running to me after meeting her and was very excited. "*Oma* (Mother)," Song-Mee said, "Belkis is Korean! She has black hair!" Until she was seven years old, Song-Mee continued to classify people by their hair color.

In some ways, she was scientifically correct—or at least as incorrect as almost everybody else. In anthropological terms, race as a concept based on skin color doesn't exist. The criteria for the classification of the human species is arbitrary and often contradictory. Pick a hair color in any classroom, and you might have three so-called "races" of red, brown, and blond students. Use skin color as the indicator, and many Brazilians would be in the same category as Egyptians. If we used blood types for classification, we would be divided into "races" of A, B, or O types. The bottom line is that if we rely on scientific evidence, race as a biological phenomenon does not exist at all.

However, racism does exist as a social evil, sometimes with deadly consequences. This challenges the feminist and women's movements to take action. At the 1995 NGO Forum on Women in Beijing, women from many cultures went beyond condemning racism. They truly confronted the issue of diversity in the women's movement and turned it into a rallying cry for unity.

How different this was from only a decade before, when governments agreed on the Nairobi Forward Looking Strategies passed in 1985. In that document, various "special groups" are discussed at the end of the document, almost literally as an afterthought. These "special groups" include youth, indigenous peoples, older women, and refugees. In contrast, the 1995 Beijing Platform for Action (BPfA) emphasizes the diversity of women's needs, backgrounds, and circumstances. It recognizes that although all women may suffer discrimination as a whole, some are at a greater disadvantage than others.

Much of the credit for this shift in emphasis goes to women of color who were not content with racism mentioned as just another human rights issue. Indigenous women in particular saw racism as a key factor in the creation of their poverty and political inequality. They worked long into the night at the UN Fourth World Conference on Women to bridge the gaps between their significant cultural differences and to arrive at consensus statements.

One of the key lessons from the BPfA is that putting diversity in the limelight can help build unity. While racism and other forms of discrimination still exert their power, the international women's movement is strong and determined to counter-act. For my part, I tell my daughter that she has the right to be any color she pleases. She just should make the most of it.

Our Bodies, Our Surgically Improved Selves

Noeleen Heyzer and I walked the tropical beaches of Rio de Janeiro in a very Asian fashion, huddled under an umbrella to shield ourselves from the hot sun. We were the oddballs here. The Brazilians seem to cast aside all cover-ups on these shores. Right before us was a happy young woman, her bare roundness in what is known locally as a dental floss bikini. Her sweaty, lean back was a perfect piece of physical form. No doubt that she had a place of honor in the species of beautiful beings. Not far away, young men stood in small herds, playing games of body gazing. Tourists like us were recognizable because our jaws dropped in amazement.

At first, Brazil's blatant body cult seemed quite innocent and even fun to me. I soon learned its dark side: the less you wear, the higher the probability that your best parts are the result of a surgical makeover. Brazilian servant girls are known to spend their life savings on cosmetic surgery. It seems to be the craze: plastic surgery is sometimes used to lift the nose just a little to give it that tantalizing movie star quality, and other times is serious and costly. Breast implants are as common as the removal of unwanted bulges and a realignment of the silhouette. Plastic surgeons have become as central to beauty treatments as pedicurists and hair stylists. In the end, the operations leave you barely recognizable, which seems to be the point of it all.

Most psychologists would agree that an obsessive preoccupation with redoing the body's imperfections is a reflection of deep insecurities. Trying to live up to someone else's unattainable ideal is a sure way to undermine your self-esteem. The problem is that women internalize superficial societal ideals, then blame themselves if they come up short.

Ironic, isn't it? Even the sunbathers who are proud of their "au naturel" look may be unable to express their natural personalities. Insecurities may be so deeply internalized that any cover-up personality is welcome. All kinds of wrong "looks" are put on. Yes, it sometimes gets hot in the feminine psyche's closet. Maybe that's what brings us out to walk the beaches.

Women's views about body image and identity are poorly understood, partly because of the traditional male bias in psychological studies. We could protest against mental health treatments that traditionally judged women against male personality standards. On the other hand, we could also develop a higher standard of our own. Becoming a self that is dependent on looks is probably self-defeating. Our surgically improved bodies will eventually abide by Mother Nature's laws, sagging in all of the "wrong" places and revealing our true selves. Wouldn't it be better to put less emphasis on body image and upgrade the whole self—mental and physical?

I am reminded of a Buddhist philosopher's insight that much of the chaos in the world reflects a similar state in the human mind. If human beings expect to promote harmony with nature, they must surely come to better terms with their first ecology: their bodies. For women, that means becoming more self-confident and setting their own standards. For men, the solution is surely the same.

A Child of the Twenty-first Century

Mazin Gabriel Kanafani, my nephew's first child, was born on August 21 at 11:30 pm. A slight 6 pounds and 13 ounces, the baby was nevertheless an evolutionary wonder, combining Arab, Korean, and German-American traits into a single DNA power pack.

Upon his birth, everyone could see that he was the most beautiful child in the world, but we struggled to decipher his family resemblances. His father claimed that his softly curved nose, oval ears, and determined mouth were from the Kanafani Palestinian blood line. Rising to the challenge, I pressed my sister—Mazin's great-aunt—to make sure that the Korean side of the family also staked its claim. However, except for his warm skin tone, my sister could not find a single feature that resembled her own. His dark brown eyes seemed like possible candidates, but they turned bluer every day.

Arguing that looks aren't everything, I scrambled for the anthropological angle. I was sure that many excellent features from our Korean ancestors were embedded in young Mazin's genetic code. For example, he must have inherited the genes for cold adaptation that North Asians have developed through natural selection. The fatty lay-

• Mazin with his grandmother

er under the skin and slightly recessed eyes will be a great advantage for survival, particularly if he has to migrate on foot with animal herds across the Bering Straits. This argument had barely landed when counterbids from Mazin's mother's family, the Orshelns, poured in. They declared that the baby's light brown curly locks came from their hearty Northern European-Germanic line. We all agreed on that point.

Growing up in America with multiple cultural identities will prove challenging for Mazin. His father always respected his own Islamic heritage, but his son will be raised as a Christian like many Arab-Americans. Mazin's parents hope that their boy will live up to his name Gabriel, meaning "strength of God." The first signs of this were promising. In his first photo shoot, he resembled a Buddha with his eyes closed and long fingers folded into a prayer.

His family outings will include typical American holidays, like Christmas, Thanksgiving, and Halloween, although he may encounter an unusual linguistic jumble. My brother's grandchildren only understand Korean. Mazin's paternal uncle's children, who once lived in Denmark, speak Danish better than English. While communications across language barriers will prove trying, Mazin will enjoy the culinary variety of his multicultural family. He will be treated to Thanksgiving turkey dinners that will include a diverse array of dishes, like Lebanese kibbe, Korean kimchi, and a Scandinavian dessert.

If he becomes curious about the dynamics between the "foreigners" in his family, I will tell him that some of his relatives were independent pioneers. They placed love above racial and religious differences and courageously trespassed across cultural borders. Psychologists could easily predict a looming adolescent crisis, but this mixed bag of identities should not be seen as a liability. Quite the contrary; it is a precious gift of global citizenship, a birthright that puts Mazin in the social avant-garde of the 21st century.

Someday, he may travel in faraway lands, looking for his roots. He will smile when the family contest of claims begins again. His relatives in the Middle East, Europe, and Asia will all greet the young American with open arms and say, "Welcome home."

Feminism and Faith

Feminists often respond to political events as emergencies, not unlike firefighters rushing to the rescue. Calls for help on urgent matters such as dowry deaths and climate change light up the NGOs' switchboards. The responses are swift and often effective, yet there remains a backlog of issues. Ethics and spirituality are among the most serious that have been put aside. Many feminists would agree that these intangibles are the essential elements of raising awareness and personal commitment, but few feminists volunteer to give these topics the attention that they deserve. If you asked an average French feminist for her thoughts about religion and women's futures, she is likely to respond, "What does faith got to do with it?"

The answer might be different if we asked women from Brazil or Argentina. The secular branch of the Latin American women's movement has been forced to admit that religion has a lot to do with feminist politics. Women in fundamentalist movements have steadily grown in influence, fanning fiery international controversies in the process such as those surrounding early menstrual regulation. Many Roman Catholic women, even some Protestant and Muslim women,

• Pramila Patten, me, Lopa Banerjee and Catharine Stimpson (2019)

have supported legislation to imprison women who have had abortions. This broad coalition rally under the banner of "family values" that upholds traditional gender roles. Ultimately, fundamentalism tests a woman's willingness to be obedient without question to husbands, fathers, or religious authority figures.

This is no trivial power play. I am concerned that such values are gaining a large following partly because they fill a personal void. Our quarrel with institutional religions has been so entangled in opposition politics that we may have neglected our own spiritual challenge.

A small group of women has veered from this secular trend. For example, women in Pakistan and Tunisia are reinterpreting Islamic doctrine to uphold women's rights. Buddhist women have worked in the women's movement for years. Within the Catholic Church, dissidents advocating for reproductive rights have rebelled against papal authority on other issues, like women in the clergy. These dedicated women have been active in the international movement, but their religiosity has not always been welcomed into the secular mainstream.

Years ago, at a meeting on the Earth Charter in Boston, I saw a glimmer of hope. The participants at the Boston Research Center meeting called "Women and the Earth Charter" came from both religious and secular women's groups. These groups exchanged views on a wide range of questions as broad as "Why do we live?" to "How do we relate to nature?" and "Where does a women's perspective fit in?"

"In the Philippine tradition, we have a saying," said former director of the Earth Council and the founder of the Earth Charter initiative Maximo Kalaw said. "In each and every person, there is a 'looh', an inner self where the heavens and the earth come together. This is the only space where one can speak a truth for all."

The group delved into topics that were not often discussed at feminist meetings, such as inner and outer harmony, spiritual balance, and ethics. We defined religion in our own terms—not as patriarchal institution, but as beliefs and values.

If spirituality is measured by the strength of one's faith in life's creation, then I believe that the international women's movement is one of the most spiritual experiences of the century. Either that, or we are all unhinged. The facts suggest that women have little cause to hope. Nevertheless, whether we are atheists or God-lovers, we ultimately believe that good triumphs over evil.

Faith has everything to do with feminism. It is only a matter of correctly defining our terms. We should bypass the traditional notion of institutional religion and focus more on the inner life. Women have nurtured and empowered a spirit that affirms an irrational faith in the goodness of humanity. In a world that is quickly losing hope, that could make all the difference.

How to Peel an Onion without Crying

I am a global citizen who has worked for the United Nations most of my life. My work has taken me to every continent. I talk about countries as if they were people, and I keep track of ten world clocks on my iPhone. In the past 12 months, I have attended meetings in Geneva with the World Health Organization and joined demonstrations at the Conference of the Parties meeting at the Paris Climate Change conference. Last month, I helped train women's organizations in Cairo, Nairobi, and Beirut.

In every country I have visited, I have to answer the question, "Who are you?" You might think that the answer is simple. But if you are working in remote rural areas of Africa or Latin America and you look like me, the answer gets pretty long.

Me: *I am the UNICEF consultant.*
Rural woman leader: *Yes, but where are you from?*
Me: *I live in Hoboken, New Jersey.*
Rural woman leader: *No, where are you* ***really*** *from?*
Me: *Oh, I was born in Pyongyang, North Korea, but I grew up in Ann*

• In Japan they think I'm from India

Arbor, Michigan.
(Here, I do the "hand thing" to show the shape of Michigan.)

Truth is, no matter what I said about originally being from Korea, most villagers in Africa or Latin America that I met would be talking the next day about this Chinese UN official they met. What have I learned as a global citizen about who I am? I am an onion with many layers of identities. Some are true, some are even imagined by myself—and many are just wrong. The real me is somewhat hard to define because it is evolving all of the time. The real me is—from one situation to another—subject to change.

When we are born, we obviously have no control over our identity. According to Korean tradition, my grandfather gave me my name in Chinese characters that means "peace forever." In many ways, growing up was a process of defining more and more of my own identity. Throughout high school, I was the prime achiever as a cheerleader, vice-president of my class, and art editor of my yearbook. Then came the rebellious years of my university days as an anti-Vietnam War activist. Long days and late nights were spent raising money to get my friends out of the Washtenaw County Jail. That was when I nearly failed an anthropology class. The one constant theme in this part of my life—in varying phases—was that I was a student.

Then came abrupt changes in my life [that] was my transition from student learner to teacher. This transition from university to work can be very jarring. One day, you are the student, asking the tough questions someone else is supposed to answer. The next day, you are the grown-up who is supposed to have the answers. I remember the first time some introduced me as an anthropologist. Was that really me now? It was—and there was no turning back.

My life in anthropology didn't get off to a happy start. I couldn't stick with a teaching job in East Lansing, Michigan because I couldn't imagine myself settling into a professor's life. It seemed like a very confining space, one that might close doors to the real world. I had lived in the United States most of my life, but my universe—the one I really lived in—was the whole world. Reading helped me imagine myself in French villages, the Trobriand Islands, and Thai villages.

I wanted to change that world hands-on and not just by writing books. When I really dug deep into my emotions and wondered where I would be happiest, I realized that I had to try to work at the United Nations. I was trying to match what was inside with how I would spend the rest of my work life. Where would I start this international journey? Even though I didn't speak Korean, I packed my bags and left to teach at Ewha Womans University. Korea, after all, was where I started my life and where I might just find a new one.

I had an interesting experience during my early days, teaching at Ewha Womans University as a Senior Fulbright Scholar. One day, my soon-to-be husband and I decided to go the U.S. Army base to have dinner. He is my biological opposite—over 6 feet tall, blond, and of Anglo-Irish descent so there was no doubt that he was a blue-blooded American.

When we got to the gate, the guard looked as us, ignored Rick, and never even asked him for proof to enter the compound. Instead, he turned to me and asked me for my venereal disease card. At that time, I guessed that this ID was required of Korean prostitutes visiting the army base to prove that they were disease-free. I was totally puzzled, but I showed him the only ID I was carrying with me that allowed me to enter the grounds. It was a Fulbright U.S. Embassy pass with my photo on it. The guard let us in.

Here's another case of mistaken identity that was not as funny. In the 1970s, I was travelling to Jordan with a Palestinian couple in my new French car. At that time, all of the borders were heavily guarded because a Japanese woman traveling with a Palestinian couple driving in a foreign car had bombed a hotel in Amman the week before. When we got to the Jordanian border, I rolled down my car window to give the soldier my passport, and suddenly, we found ourselves surrounded by armed guards, guns pointed at our heads. They made us get out of the car, and for the rest of the day, they stripped my car nearly bare, tore out the lining of its doors, took out the back seat, and opened every bottle and package they could find in my luggage.

When I asked why we were being detained, I was told something I will never forget. The enraged soldier holding my passport, waving it in my face, said, "This is a fake passport. You are obviously Egyptian." I was an Egyptian terrorist in the company of a Palestinian couple, on my way to bomb another hotel in Amman. We got out of this mess only because my friend was an officer in the Jordanian Air Force. By evening, someone came to our rescue.

So, I know how it feels to have a serious disconnect between my

Indigenous peoples caucus – Rio (2002)

real identity and what others think of me. What is the one lesson to learn from this? Even if you can't change how others see you, you can decide what you make of it. Will you be utterly destroyed? Is your identity totally wrapped up in what work you do? What defines your worth? I think one of the hardest battles in life to hold on tight to our own identities no matter how many times our jobs may change.

If you are wondering what to do with all these layers, try to peel your onion. I promise you can do this without crying. In fact, it may even make you happy. Being a global citizen means that sometimes you peel away all layers of nationality, age, ethnicity, and even gender until you reach the core as a human being.

When I held a UN laissez-passer (the UN equivalent of a passport), I travelled as a UN citizen, not as an American. I had to think and act on behalf of every man, woman, and child in every culture, on earth. I had to stand up for human rights, and my responsibility was to make choices fit for all of humanity.

In the development work I have done, whether digging water wells with UNICEF or advising governments about women, health and tobacco, my sense of purpose was always focused on how the UN could bring hope and dignity to those it served. Ultimately, what we strive for as global citizens is to give everyone a chance and a right to discover and fulfill their own potential, free from prejudice, poverty, and violence. What we wish for everyone is the right to define their own identity.

Everyone can peel away his or her layers of identities. At the opening of the NGO Forum during the UN Fourth World Conference on Women in Beijing in 1995, I looked around the stadium at the faces of 20,000 women and men, boys and girls, and asked myself, 'What are they doing here? Why have they come?' For the next few weeks of that meeting, I looked for my answer—and then I found it.

One day, I walked into a tent at the NGO Forum and saw a group of women dancing the hokey pokey. These women could not understand each other's languages. They came from different religions and cultures; they were different ethnicities and ages. But there they were, celebrating their oneness as women. They had stripped away all identities until they found a common one, and they had done this on purpose of their own free will. Somehow, through this gathering of fairly ordinary women, victims changed their identities to advocates. Those who thought they were alone felt connected to millions of women around the world. And the international women's movement gained a momentum that cannot be stopped to this day.

So, you can see why I like being an onion. We have the power to change our identities, but we also have the power to help others be true to theirs. My parting words to you who wish to make the world a better place is this: if you want to change the world, learn more about who you are—and who you can be.

Chapter 3

Violence against Women

"The issue of gender disparities is ultimately one of disparate freedoms."

_ Amartya Sen, Nobel Prize Laureate

Introduction

When women are free from violence, they exercise their voice and help change the public agenda. This isn't just rhetoric. We have good proof. When American women lawmakers turned their attention to child and maternal health, infant mortality rates dropped to 15 percent. (World Development Report-Gender Equality, World Bank, 2012).

It took many years for violence against women and girls to be understood. Not long ago, we talked about the silent and private agony of battered women in the home. Today, we argue that violence is a cultural problem, a societal pathology that takes other insidious forms: rape during conflicts, female genital mutilation, forced early marriage, sex trafficking, sexual harassment, and femicide. Many groups such as indigenous women, women and girls living with disabilities, the homeless, widows, and women and girls living with HIV/AIDS face multiple discriminations. The same is true for many migrant and internally displaced women, refugees, women in the military and incarcerated women. These complexities have made it hard for us to see the common denominator: unequal power relations be-

Protests at the NGO Forum in Beijing (1995)

tween men and women.

One of the most powerful and least expensive ways to prevent violence against women and girls is for the world's leaders to consistently and publicly say that it is wrong. For example, university presidents have to be more vocal about ending rape and sexual harassment on campus. Some men have already set a good example. In May 2013, President Obama stepped forward to support same-sex marriage. At that time, no laws were passed, and no enforcements were in place. However, with his public and very visible announcement, the terms of the national debate were changed. These actions helped to redefine what is acceptable male behavior and made all the difference.

We also have to be smarter about why small-scale projects aren't working. Violence against women can't be solved by a few school educational programs or public campaigns. We could have shelters for battered women on every city street corner, but that still wouldn't be safe for families. Our approach has to be a comprehensive package targeted at unraveling patriarchal privilege at the core.

There is one glaring gap in our knowledge about prevention. We need to know more about why some boys become perpetrators while the majority of men do not. Why do boys who experience violence in their childhood home grow up to batter their spouses and children? Why do men who have experienced childhood traumas and conflicts survive and become advocates for ending violence against women and girls? Without a global, multi-country study that identifies risks, protective factors, and causes for men and boys, we are left in the dark about how to tackle prevention and when it must be implemented in the men's life cycle.

I think the UN is an ideal place to tackle the issue globally because violence against women and girls is the most universal and pervasive kind of human rights violation. The founding principles of the UN include development and peace for all women and men equally as a human right. I have great respect for the many UN policies and legal instruments on hand, like the Convention on the Elimination of All forms of Discrimination against Women (CEDAW) and its Optional Protocol. These instruments carry the weight of the world's opinion and are the beginnings of policy and legal reforms at national levels. They are our main tools of defining standards of justice and social norms. Let's begin to leverage the power of global consensus.

Singing for the Dead

During a recent visit to Botswana, a friend invited me to participate in the funeral rites of her cousin. Abandoned by a husband who had abused her for most of her life, the deceased woman had raised five children alone.

We arrived at the mortuary where her children were waiting. The nearest of kin went inside to fetch the body. In accordance with tradition, the deceased woman's maternal uncle acted as the head of the family and took charge of the rituals. During the ceremony, he didn't mention that she had died from AIDS, but everyone knew that some of the children might also be infected. If so, their only hope would be the government's new program to give antiretroviral drugs to everyone with HIV/AIDS.

However, a funeral was not an appropriate occasion to talk about AIDS. It was time for kinsmen to send her joyfully into the next world and for the ancestors to welcome the woman into their realm. I joined in the feasting. A teenager with beautiful round eyes and a warm voice was seated next to me. She adjusted her scarf just enough to reveal severe burn marks on the right side of her face.

• Unity Dow in Botswana (2017)

"A group of hoodlums threw her on a barbeque pit," a woman explained. The girl nodded, showing me the dark grill marks on her right arm, thigh, and leg.

"I don't know why they did this to me, except that I talked back to them when they were rude," the girl said. Other women shared their horror stories. Some women never felt safe, no matter the time or place. Violence was a constant threat behind sexual coercion. Girls contracted AIDS because they were powerless to defend themselves against older men who believed in the superstition that virgins could cure them.

Not so long ago, one third of Botswana's females ages 15 to 24 were infected with HIV/AIDS. Although rates have declined, violence associated with alcohol abuse remains a social problem of epidemic proportions.

This isn't a scenario that unfolds only in Africa. Violence against women and girls is a global phenomenon. It is a societal pathology that takes a variety of malevolent and deadly forms in many cultures across many classes. It is the most prevalent violation of women's human rights globally and a major reason women and girls do not feel safe at home or in the streets. In the United States, there is a strong link between intimate partner violence and HIV. For example, women in relationships with violence have four times the risk for contracting sexually transmitted diseases than women in relationships without violence.

Gender-based violence is also an urgent economic and social development issue. According to the World Health Organization report in 2019, domestic violence and rape rank higher than cancer, motor vehicle accidents, war, and malaria in the global estimates of risk factors for women. Domestic and sexual violence and the associated costs in the United Kingdom alone costs the country £5.7 billion per year. In the United States, the health care cost of intimate partner rape, physical assault, and stalking totals $5.8 billion each year, nearly $4.1 billion of which is for direct medical and mental health care services. Lost productivity from paid work and household chores and lifetime earnings lost by homicide victims totals nearly $1.8 billion.[1]

What is the UN doing about this? The UN Secretary General, supported by UN Women, has taken the lead, engaging men and boy to end violence against women and combat gender-based violence. At the UN Commission on the Status of Women meeting in 2013, hundreds of NGOs gathered together to prevent and end violence against women and girls. In its Agreed Conclusions (a consensus document that provides policy guidance for the UN and governments), the Commission strongly condemns violence against women and girls and notes the important role that men and boys can have in prevention.

1 *Costs of Intimate Partner Violence against Women in the United States*, United States Department of Health and Human Services, 2003.

I plan to return to Botswana very soon to catch up on some good news. I heard that the Harvard AIDS Initiative is working closely with the government to combat date rape and other forms of violence against women and girls as part of their HIV/AIDS prevention program. Let us hope that combined effort between social reform and health can make a difference.

Breaking the Silence on Women's Human Rights[1]

Every year, women around the world celebrate 16 Days of Activism against Gender Violence starting on November 25, International Day against Violence against Women, and lasting through December 10, International Human Rights Day. Like musicians improvising in a global concert, women trumpet their issues and create a resonant noise. The political rhythms vary, but the themes are loud and clear. Women's rights are human rights. Violence against women in all its forms must end.

Why are these campaigns so important? For centuries, violence has been—and for many women still is—a constant threat. Indian Sati, or the burning of widows on funeral pyres, sacrificed women for the sake of family pride, and no one called it a crime. British common law declared it legal to beat your wife as long as you did so with a stick "no thicker than your thumb." The rape of women and girls was con-

1 Based on an article authored by Charlotte Bunch and Soon-Young Yoon titled "Women—The Long, Long Journey" that was published in *The Earth Times*.

• The Pacific women shine in Beijing (1995)

sidered a soldier's just prize, a side issue to the tragedies of war. Such abuses were kept hidden and trivialized. Violence was a personal shame that most women hid. It was not understood as a human rights violation worthy of international attention by the United Nations.

Many of these abuses still occur. Customs and law sanction honor killings of women. Religious leaders condone the infibulation of girls as a justifiable mean to give men pleasure. The UN and governments are starting to redress these abuses thanks to Security Council resolution 1325 and actions of the Committee on the Elimination of All Forms of Discrimination against Women (CEDAW). Additional advances were made when CEDAW issued a new General Recommendations that requires governments to report on women in conflict and post-conflict situations as well as the women's access to justice. The Beijing Platform for Action, adopted in 1995, outlines recommendations to ensure human rights literacy for women to know their human rights and also spelled out policy actions on violence against women and situations of armed conflict.

The credit for the UN's actions goes to the women's movement. In the last half century, activism reached a critical mass that was reflected in the UN's decision to call for an International Women's Year in 1975 followed by a UN Decade for Women and four UN world conferences on women. The UN world conferences of the 1990s served as global town meetings where women exchanged ideas across the boundaries of culture and nationality and brought their experiences to bear on the global agendas of those events. For many women, these meetings also provided the first opportunities to meet together internationally.

Women organized events and hearings to expose violations of their rights and formed caucuses regionally and internationally. They also prepared documents that introduced women's human rights perspectives to the agendas of many UN conferences, including the Earth Summit in Rio de Janeiro, the World Conference on Human Rights in Vienna, the International Conference on Population and Development in Cairo, the Social Summit in Copenhagen, the Habitat Conference in Istanbul, and the Fourth World Women's Conference in Beijing. Women have since rallied to hold governments accountable at follow-up UN events, such as Beijing Plus 20 in New York in 2020. These events and caucuses have moved women's concerns beyond the women's conferences and provided a powerful voice for women on many global issues, such as the Small Arms Treaty and international crime.

Women around the world broke the silence with their actions. They have found a common language of liberation and helped the UN and governments look at the world through women's eyes. Women's groups have shown that a nonviolent social movement for change can be revolutionary and that there are peaceful means to ending violence. They have also established that the world vision for peace cannot be achieved as long as there is a reign of terror against women and girls.

What Women Have in Common with Camels

Once while visiting quarries near the Egyptian pyramids, a scruffy stone worker gave long, hard looks to me and my companion. I thought his looks were just signs of curiosity, but they turned out to mean much more. He stopped his work and proposed to buy me with the help of a translator. In between the misunderstandings about the exact price, there was something about how white and straight my teeth were. Fortunately, my partner wasn't short of cash, and he declined the offer.

Later, I learned from my Egyptian friends that I had experienced something fairly common in rural areas in other parts of the world: evaluating a potential bride by her teeth. According to my friends, women's teeth indicate their age and health status. It seems that teeth are also considered a private, sensual part of the body. I was less amused when they told me that traders used similar physical standards to price camels.

This experience did little to lower my self-esteem. However, it did remind me that women and girls are traded like animals on the market in many societies. The trafficking of women and children has

• The camel and me

emerged as one of the darker sides of globalization; a flourishing criminal underground network uses new information technologies to violate, rather than defend, human rights. Boys and young men are also victims of forced labor and sex trafficking.

Controls on the illegal flow of sex workers have been complicated by the increases in international migration. In the last decade, the number of females leaving to seek work abroad has increased at a faster rate than that of men, particularly from countries whose economies have suffered. Moreover, many women are migrating alone as temporary workers in low paid jobs and are vulnerable to employment scams that are fronts for the sex slave trade.

The UN Office on Drugs and Crime, in cooperation with other UN agencies, is taking action to protect international migrants while opening borders for easier movement of labor. Its efforts are admirable, but the real problem for women and girls goes beyond labor standards and fair wages. The culprits are international criminals who use legitimate open markets to traffic organs, drugs, tobacco, and people for lucrative profit. Let us keep our focus on law enforcement and criminal justice, not just migration policies and labor practices.

What's Optional about the Optional Protocol?

Many of us are signing up for self-taught crash courses on law and treaties. With terms like "optional protocol" floating around, we have to become on-the-spot legal experts or lose track of key debates. The demystification of professional language is absolutely necessary, even desirable, when it comes to issues like violence against women. The Optional Protocol of the Convention on the Elimination of All Forms of Discrimination against Women (CEDAW) can enhance women's political presence only after it has been unfolded from UN baggage and made to fit the average person.

As I understand it, the document gives women a means to enforce CEDAW with a procedure for complaints. I found that many of my friends shared my misconceptions. When I first heard about the Optional Protocol, I was quite confused. My first question was: what is optional about the Optional Protocol? I assumed that it would be a useful "escape" clause, allowing governments to qualify their commitments to CEDAW's provisions and make it less binding, otherwise optional. In fact, this is way off the mark. The document is supposed to give CEDAW bigger teeth.

I also misunderstood the use of protocol in this instance. I assumed that it would contain significant statements about the importance of women's rights. Wrong again. Much to my surprise, the document was almost entirely about the rules by which complaints can be lodged and how to respond.

Below are some lessons that I have learned about the Optional Protocol:

Lesson #1: Governments that have signed and ratified CEDAW have the option of adopting this additional process. Signing the Optional Protocol was a sign of sincerity and opened the way to self-criticism. It would also grant a higher enforcement influence to the Commission on the Status of Women (CSW) and more weight to the words of the CEDAW document.

Lesson #2: The Optional Protocol is not about new rights. It is about how to make violations known. It describes who can file, how to do it properly, and other such operational details. Individual women or possibly groups may take their own governments to task and make their cases known to the CSW.

Lesson #3: Since the Optional Protocol is subordinate to CEDAW, only those countries that have signed and ratified the convention will be allowed to sign onto this portion. Unfortunately, this means that there is no possibility that the United States will be a party to this document. This is a loss for American advocates to end violence against women and girls.

Lesson #4 is yet to be learned. That lesson is how to finance, manage, and respond quickly to a barrage of cases. With the majority of the world's poor women deprived of the rights to adequate food, safe water, and clean environment, the complaints concerning economic rights alone should create an instant backlog.

With this in mind, it is essential that governments provide funding for human rights education on how to access national and regional mechanisms before reaching the CSW. In the long run, human rights should not be the sole responsibility of the legal systems but part of good global citizenship.

Child Prostitutes

Violence against girls includes crimes that threaten their mental and physical health. Children trafficked into prostitution are among the most vulnerable. Furthermore, in countries like Nepal, the AIDS epidemic is a serious threat to girls who are lured into prostitution. Fueled by booming tourism, the criminal trafficking of women and girls has driven more than 200 thousand women and children into sexual slavery. The most vulnerable are the members of remote hill tribes and lower castes, both of which provide a steady stream of sex workers into the market. In addition to sexual slavery at home, girls are sold as child brides across the border in India.

At a meeting of the Committee on the Elimination of All Forms of Discrimination against Women (CEDAW), the secretary of Nepal's Ministry for Law and Justice Terth Man Shakya noted that his country's borders were difficult to patrol. He explained that the prostitution problem started when women from hill areas were brought to Kathmandu as housemaids. In hard times, employers released them from domestic work and turned them over to brothels. A bill to control trafficking was passed in 1986, making the offense punishable by

• UN Vienna anti-trafficking display (2016)

15 years' imprisonment, but the situation has worsened.

Child prostitutes are in greater demand than ever before because of the mistaken notion that they are less likely to be infected. Virgins are presented at high prices to brothel clients as AIDS-free. They are exploited, and many become pregnant. Abortion laws do not allow them to terminate pregnancies without parental approval, a condition impossible for these girls to meet. Thus, 14-year-old girls run the risk of bearing HIV-infected children or dying in childbirth.

The government has tried to take charge of the situation by gathering evidence. The first two HIV-positive cases among Nepalese women were identified in 1989. Since then, many more HIV-positive women have been identified in comparison to HIV-positive men. However, the rates of infection among children and girls in sexual slavery is almost unknown. With few hospitals and the high costs of detection, no one knows for sure how many child prostitutes will die from the virus.

CEDAW recommended that the Nepalese government enforce stricter laws to protect the rights of girls against rape, violence, and prostitution. The South Asia Association for Regional Cooperation (SAARC) Summit held in Kathmandu also introduced a convention on trafficking in girls and children. These measures, along with the recommendations of the UN General Assembly, are essential steps toward protecting the future of girls like those in Nepal. The international community must be alerted to the plight of these children whose daily lives are a gamble with violence surrounding AIDS.

The Truth about Gender-based Violence

On December 10, 1997, Ana Parejo Vivar went on Spanish television to reveal how her husband had abused her. Then, much to his surprise, she announced that she was seeking a divorce. Ten days later, her husband doused her with gasoline and set her on fire. Death was a high price to pay for speaking out, but she would not hide in terror. That year, 17 thousand cases of domestic violence were recorded, and only five percent of women went to the police. By 2010, Spanish courts had passed 145 thousand sentences against male aggressors (*The New York Times*, February 23, 2011). More women are seeking and getting justice—and that is a healthy trend.

Courageous women around the world have declared that gender violence should not be a guarded secret, and they look increasingly to the media to help them expose its malignancy. Fortunately, there are signs that mass media is paying attention. Many television producers now regard the rape of women refugees in Eastern Europe and Africa as legitimate war stories equal in importance to the siege of a city. Newspaper editors have listed domestic violence stories in their crimes section, a step up from the traditional attitude that these sto-

• FIRE radio broadcasts (1995)

ries were not newsworthy. Moved by tragic accounts, well-meaning journalists even portray the sordid details of fatal beatings. We are horrified by the assaults. We grit our teeth and swear we will do something to help.

However, does reporting about gender violence inspire action? I suspect keeping the public eye on the problem raises awareness, but also merely tantalizes our sympathy. Just the facts may not be enough to stir the average citizen out of complacency. Reports of gender violence buttress the false notion that men's nature is naturally savage, brutish, and nearly uncontrollable. The public can even develop a depressing attitude of indifference because there is little in the news that shows a way out of these situations.

The remedy is that we need more good news. By good, I don't mean sugarcoated tales that ignore what's wrong. There has to be more nuanced reporting between tales of misery and upbeat stories about women's leadership, activities, and progress. The truth is that women aren't just victims. They have mobilized for years to fight gender violence and are making important gains. The stories that need more coverage are the ones that show how the UN, governments, judges, police, and doctors are making a difference in partnership with local men and women's groups. That kind of news encourages citizens to take action.

Alas, many of the wonderful news groups like *FIRE* and the International Women's Tribune Center have been lost, and more effort must be placed on funding feminist media. Women's media like the Women's UN Report Network (WUNRN) is an online resource for feminist news. There is a lot of buzz these days about the international campaign known as the 16 Days of Activism Against Gender Violence. This global event has become so popular that many governments have become official sponsors.

Men are also getting more involved in combating gender violence. Canadian men are showing their commitment by wearing white ribbons, signing petitions, and making donations to support women's shelters. Breakthrough, an award-winning grass-roots campaign, reaches millions of men and boys who ring the bell to end violence against women and girls. The media need to pay more attention to these kinds of events because the bad news about gender violence is only half of the whole truth. The rest is about hope.

Children under Fire

In the 1970s, many children in Lebanon were born, raised, and died in a decade of total war. Like kids in Detroit, Michigan, who can identify car models by their engine noises, Lebanese children played games to see who could tell the difference between one kind of gunshot and another. Many of them had an additional skill: how to distinguish firecrackers from machine gun fire within the first few bursts. Even these imaginative escapes had their limits. Children missed the simple pleasures of peacetime, like going out into the streets safely. Outbreaks of fighting during the day kept children from going to school. Some never went at all.

Although women's groups and peace organizations tried to cross over enemy lines to establish peace, other leaders organized children to make sure the hostilities endured. Before his assassination, I learned about this first-hand from Bashir Gemayel, former head of the radical Christian party. Through special arrangements, I secured a tour of East Beirut with him at the wheel and armed guards in the back seat. To dodge possible car bombs, we changed cars several times before we arrived at our final destination. A fanatic militarist leader, he was

• Bangladesh child

proud of his plan to raise the next generation of loyal youth for what he thought was a holy war. We stopped in front a school with students in their early teens lined up in smart, scout-like uniforms.

"This is my next army," he announced. He had realized that the wars could continue long enough for this to happen.

Distorting children's impressionable minds to sway political allegiance has been a common strategy of dictators. Unfortunately, recruiting children into armies is also becoming more widespread. UNICEF (https://www.unicef.org) estimates that some 300 thousand children under the age of 18 are involved in more than 30 conflicts worldwide. In many parts of the world, children as young as eight and ten years of age have been forcibly recruited, coerced, or induced to become combatants. Other grave violations include killing and maiming of children, attacks against schools, and denial of humanitarian access for children.

Lest we think that this only affects boys; up to 10 percent of children carrying arms are girls. The Convention on the Elimination of All Forms of Discrimination against Women (CEDAW) General Recommendation on Women and Girls in Conflict and Post Conflict is a welcome legal instrument. Pramila Patten, CEDAW expert and then-chair of the working group for the General Recommendation, hopes that it will help to protect girls from being kidnapped by armies as well as help them to reintegrate into their communities once they return. The UN's Office of the Special Representative of the Secretary-General for Children and Armed Conflict was established in 2012 to give a moral voice and prominence to the rights and protection of children affected by armed conflict.

As part of preventing violence against women and girls, we must also pay more attention to what happens to boys during wartime. In countries with prolonged civil strife, such as in Sierra Leone, many children have missed the chance to go to school and develop precious ties with classmates. Instead, they might have been involved in demonstrations or have even gone to jail.

Often, children don't have to be coerced to join armies. They volunteer because there are no options, no schools, and no jobs. Without schools to bond youth together, boys can easily be attracted to renegade groups and gangs that give them a sense of belonging. Even if they are lucky enough to attend school, they may not learn the values that would rescue them from a cycle of violence. We all know that childhood experiences help shape adult worlds. Many of us had our chances. Shouldn't these children also have theirs?

Female Genital Mutilation— Who Should Lead the Way?

In the early days of the campaign against female genital mutilation (FGM), a French women's group circulated a petition protesting the practice at an international meeting on women and development in Dakar. They had heard their African sisters' stories about how young girls were infibulated, their entire private parts removed and sewn back together. This extreme form of FGM-induced psycho-physical trauma in girls would endure their entire lives. In the case of infibulation, re-cutting would have to take place before intercourse and cause more physical pain and injury with each childbirth. The French participants were so outraged that they called for a ban on the practice.

As the petition reached me, my Ethiopian friend Belkis whispered to me to not sign it. She felt strongly that African women should take the leadership on this issue because Westerners might misunderstand the practice. In her experience, FGM was sensationalized, associated with so-called "barbaric" African practices and taken out of its cultural context.

The African women raised their voices in protest and brought the petition signing to a dead halt. The French women were shocked at this resistance and insisted that collective action was the only answer. The African women would have no part of their initiative. Resisting the French feminist call for action, the Africa group started their own movement. At that meeting, the first pan-African NGO association against FGM was organized and was called the Inter-African Committee on Traditional Practices Affecting the Health of Women and Children.

That meeting was decades ago, but it is important to remember that choice of leadership is still an issue. FGM is a heinous violent act against girls, but it cannot be eradicated unless those who are fighting for change understand the deeply-entrenched beliefs of the people who practice it.

Whether the movement against FGM is in the Sudan, Senegal, France, or Germany, the women who have to live with the political realities of banning FGM should lead the way. They are the most knowledgeable about the political landmines, the evolving cultural contexts, and how local women react to outside involvement. At the same time, when international action is needed, sisters from around the world should be ready to help.

Women who want to show support for the African women's cause can often contribute by learning about their own governments' positions at international meetings on FGM. These women can also be advocates for foreign policies that are a combination of non-interference and unwavering financial support for women's sexual and reproductive rights as a human right. Respect for diversity requires us to share leadership, and the women's movement is learning these lessons the hard way. In some countries, it is taking time. Once the lessons are under our belts, we'll be qualified to teach others.

Making Governments Accountable for Sexual Violence

On July 18, 2011, the Convention on the Elimination of All Forms of Discrimination against Women (CEDAW) had a General Discussion Day at its 49th session to launch the drafting of an important General Recommendation. This document would focus on women and girls in conflict prevention, conflict, and post-conflict. A general recommendation document was needed because governments had failed to report on conflicts. If countries did not report, how could CEDAW be used to help victims seek justice?

To build the legal framework, CEDAW experts needed solid data. Unfortunately, there was very little research that accurately portrayed the situation of the victims. For the first time in CEDAW's history, this gap was to be filled through regional consultations with Pramila Patten, the Secretary General's Special Representative on Sexual Violence in Conflict who was also serving as the lead CEDAW expert for this topic at the time. At her suggestion, I traveled as an NGO observer to regional consultations. I was anxious to learn more about how CEDAW could make a difference to the survivors of violence.

These regional meetings gave us important insights into the chal-

CEDAW experts: Nicole Ameline and Bandana Rana (2016)

lenges facing CEDAW in Africa, the Arab States, Asia, South and Eastern Europe, and Central Asia. As the meetings progressed, I watched the scope, the definitions, and the concepts of the General Recommendation draft evolve and grow in response. It was like watching a skilled potter create a new vessel from clay—and I was fascinated.

What did I learn? I discovered in those meetings how important it is to build a bridge between those you seek to protect and the legal instrument you craft on their behalf. That distance can be very long. CEDAW General Recommendations are like encrypted codes which may speak in highly esoteric, legal jargon enveloped in distilled theories, much like other UN documents.

Perhaps the most moving experience for me was in Guatemala. During a special session with about 20 survivors of the country's prolonged war, indigenous women described how government troops came into their villages to recruit their men for the army. When the men hid in the fields, women stayed behind to protect the children and homes. That's when soldiers went on a rampage destroying property and livelihood and committing some of the most shameful acts of sexual violence against women and girls.

We listened to the women's testimonies of sexual slavery, rapes of pregnant women, destruction of fetuses, exhibitions of mutilated women's bodies, humiliations, and forced naked dancing in front of soldiers. Rape was often a prelude to death, as it had become a part of the rituals preceding the massacres committed by the army in the highlands. These tactics were not random acts by soldiers but deliberately designed to intimidate the population. Selective sexual violence was also used to torture and repress women in social or revolutionary organizations, an approach that often became a generalized practice to punish any enemy.

What were governments in this region doing to assure women access to justice? Dr. Miran Perla Jiminez, Honorable Magistrate of the Supreme Court of Justice from El Salvador, explained that governments tried very hard to restore the strength of their judiciary systems by creating special lines of recourse for survivors. However, in her country as in Guatemala, the rising tide of international crime and the strength of armed vigilantes were unraveling possibilities for women's security. While I was there, the reports of femicide (the killing of women for their organs) and drug crime were so threatening that the minister of the interior advised all of us to return to our hotels before dark. I learned that international crime joins with local unrest to undermine the states' authority and the rule of law.

Hope comes from some countries where women's NGOs take great pride in their roles as agents to prevent conflict. Early warning systems using mobile phones, training programs for the judiciary and police, whistleblower protection laws, and witness protection programs have been put in place. These advances are a source of hope for prevention policies and programs in other regions and to the survivors I met in Guatemala.

These days, whenever I hear about a new UN Security Council resolution on sexual violence during conflict or the importance of women in peace building, I remember the faces and stories of the survivors of gender violence I have met. I believe that when we keep these faces before us, we can't help but strengthen our resolve to use every tool—legal, social or economic—in our power to prevent such injustices.

Rape as a War Crime

In 2005, former comfort woman Jang Jeom-Dol spoke at the Korea Society in New York, where she recalled her own experiences as a victim of the Japanese Imperial Army's sexual enslavement. Jang told us about how she was taken from her family when she was just 14 years old and told she was going to work in a factory. When she ended up at an official brothel in Manchuria, she attempted suicide and tried to escape. She was caught and beaten so severely that the left side of her face was permanently paralyzed. After a year and a half, she was transported to another station in Singapore. Several pregnancies ended in miscarriages during her time in the captivity. In 1945, after Japan's surrender, her captors left her and her fellow comfort women destitute and marooned thousands of miles from home. Relying on the kindness of strangers, Jang eventually returned to her village in Korea only to learn that her family had been scattered by the war.

Her story was a tangible example of the war crimes of sexual slavery during World War II. During the war in Asia, an estimated 200 thousand girls and young women—some as young as 12 years old—were abducted or coerced to become sex slaves for the Japanese army.

• Pramila Patten, Secretary-General's Special Representative on Sexual Violence in Conflict

According to one account, Korean girls were repeatedly raped, tortured, and subjected to sexual servicing for up to 100 soldiers a day. Many had multiple pregnancies, forced abortions, or were given sterilization injections. Japanese records reveal that victims were transported to comfort stations in countries throughout the Asia and Pacific region. Sex slaves were killed at the end of the war as the soldiers retreated. Those who survived lived with physical and mental disabilities for the rest of their lives.

The demonstrations and public hearings at national and international venues by former comfort women was one of the most important turning points in Korea's social history. In my eyes, this campaign symbolized the blossoming of the modern Korean women's movement and part of a global effort to handle rape and sexual slavery as war crimes. Sexual violence was put on national and international policy agendas as the international women's movement rallied to the cause. Korean politicians took notice of women's human rights abuses as a matter of national urgency.

Sexual violence in conflict zones of Africa and other regions have become the subject of increasing reports. Thousands of tragic women's stories, past and present, could not be ignored. Political action was finally taken when the UN adopted Security Council resolution 1325, recognizing rape as a war crime and appointed Pramila Patten as the Secretary-General's Special Representative on Sexual Violence in Conflict. If anyone accuses the UN of being irrelevant, its actions on this issue stand out in its favor. With the UN's support, national actions take on global significance that can help bring perpetrators to justice and give victims a pathway to justice.

Women Light the Way for Human Rights

Two young Polish women, Justyna and Paulina, stepped up to the podium at the Church Center in New York City to share their story. Their testimony stunned the audience gathered at the Global Tribunal to Celebrate and Demand Women's Human Rights. When they were only 16 years old, two men promised them their first model shoot. Instead of giving them jobs, the men drugged and abducted them to Germany and forced them into prostitution. Once freed, Justyna and Paulina eventually became university students and took their case to court, but had to face a long, slow journey to heal their psychological wounds. It was a courageous struggle that no teenager should have to face.

After they told their story, there was a hush in the dark room. A chapel was the perfect place for their testimonials; confessions and absolution are a part of its tradition. More testimonies came from women around the world, from Afghanistan to Zimbabwe to Costa Rica to South Africa: Zarghuna Waziri (a teacher from Afghanistan), Alda Facio (from the Women's Caucus for Gender Justice in the International Criminal Court), Lydia Zigomo Nyatsanza (Zimbabwe),

• Women's voices at the Beijing Women's Conference (1995)

Maria Gerardina Lopez (Costa Rica), and Palesa Beverly Ditsie (South Africa). Each of their stories broke a silence about a victim's past. Before this sympathetic and often tearful audience, they could share their tragedies and turn our attention to the need to speak out.

I have always been moved by a singular feature of these women's testimonials. They did not cry out for vengeance. Their stories had the voice of compassion, a plea for justice based on legal measures. They called for non-violent solutions: protests and legal action. I asked myself how could these women be so magnanimous after what they have experienced. It was as if they felt that revenge would be a waste of time. The need to rescue others was a much more urgent matter.

After the women spoke, the group marched outside for a candlelight vigil. We observed a minute of silence in remembrance of women who have died from gender violence. Then, the solemn mood changed to celebration as we cheered for the achievements of women who have helped light the way for human rights.

Chapter 4

Finding the Earth's Balance

"Rejoicing in the wonder and beauty of the Earth we share a reverence for life and the sources of our being…"

_ Earth Charter

Introduction

The UN has declared a climate emergency—and it is real. We must reduce greenhouse gas emissions enough to keep the earth's temperature below 1.5 degree Celsius and prevent irreversible damage to our world's ecosystems.

How can we beat the earth's clock? For years, the feminist and women's movements have argued this truth: if you want to scale up and speed up progress on any development agenda, you have to unleash the power of women's potential. When women can freely decide how many children they want, family sizes will adjust more quickly to available resources. Rural and indigenous women are particularly knowledgeable about protecting biodiversity and combatting climate change because they practice seed selection, manage forests, and make decisions about household energy use. This isn't just about human rights principles. It is applying these principals to get practical results and solve global problems.

The flip side to this argument is that gender discrimination puts the brakes on progress, particularly poverty reduction. Women are the main decision makers and workers related to water use but are

• Climate Change event in Marrakesh (2016)

poorly represented in water management. Women are critical in rebuilding communities after natural disasters, but more women than men die during those tragic times. Women produce the majority of the world's food but own less than 11 percent of the land. Imagine the hurdles they have to face in post-conflict situations to rebuild their farms. All of this adds up to one conclusion: gender inequality is bad economics and bad governance.

Women can leverage the power of global consensus documents. The women's movement needs to make sure that the Beijing Platform for Action (BPfA) works side-by-side with the Convention on the Elimination of All Forms of Discrimination against Women (CEDAW). The BPfA acts as a policy guide, and CEDAW gives it teeth as a legally binding instrument.

The CEDAW Committee took a strong position in the General Recommendation 37 stating that all stakeholders should ensure that climate change and disaster risk reduction measures are gender responsive, sensitive to indigenous knowledge systems and respect human rights. Women's right to participate at all levels of decision-making must be guaranteed in climate change policies and program.

Let's make sure that governments put gender equality and the empowerment of women and girls front and center in climate policies. These are the accelerators we need to save our planet.

Mossi Women

In the late 1970s, the Yatenga plateau in Burkina Faso was afflicted with droughts. When the rains finally came, water quickly disappeared underground and out of reach. The Mossi people longed for their ancestral times when rich trade kingdoms flourished and proud warriors were celebrated in songs. However, due to prolonged agricultural crises, many Mossi villagers became environmental refugees who were surrendering their homes to drought.

A grassroots organization called the Naam groups took matters into their own hands. Community organizers worked with youths, women, and men to create a network of community development councils until there was a Naam Federation extending over the entire region.

The Naam groups held meetings where everyone was supposed to join in the effort to save their communities. After many discussions, some women saw little progress and became exasperated.

"The men were just complaining," one woman told me. "They said there is nothing to eat. They talked about the dying cattle, deforestation, and how the young men were leaving. But no one had solutions."

As the story goes, Minata from Somiaga rose from her seat. In the

• Mossi women in Burkina Faso (1983)

midst of the passionate speeches, she said in a calm voice, "What you say is fine, but it is useless to talk about livestock and food when there is no water. The first problem is that we have no water. We women are going to find out how to get it."

When she sat down, everyone looked at each other. There was a long silence. They were amazed at how simple the solution really was. Minata's legend began from that time. She helped to organize the Naam women's groups, which took the lead in solving the water problem. The women said that they would build huge traditional dams made of mud and rocks in order to catch rainwater. Then, they would plant trees around the dams, feed the cattle, and dig gardens. This project would take days of carrying earth in baskets on their heads and moving boulders.

When the men hesitated to cooperate, the women threatened to leave their homes and return to their parents' villages. This threat got the men's attention, and they pitched in to help. Donors provided

Mossi girl carrying jug

technical help and vehicles. Naam groups that built these initial "mother dams" helped other villages build "daughter dams" until they covered the entire plateau.

The story of the Mossi women's dams illustrates the potential of what can be done when women have a say in environmental management. Yet, few national programs have learned this lesson. Some governments have focused attention on women's roles in safe drinking water and domestic water supply, but they often overlook women in other considerable issues like urban and rural infrastructure and climate change treaties.

Women's empowerment has been highlighted in consultations on the Sustainable Development Goals (SDGs) and the Post-2015 Development Agenda that will replace the Millennium Development Goals (MDGs) when they expire. UN Women and the World Bank reports advocate that gender equality should not be a side issue to environment planning. Instead, these UN bodies see it as the most strategic fix that governments can make to accelerate progress on food security, energy, sustainable cities and human settlements, land degradation, and drought.

From the micro-ecology of the home to the global ecological system, women's participation in environment management and sustainable development is essential. Women's groups should be the leaders to focus the world's attention on the right priorities. Sometimes, this has happened at large UN conferences. On other occasions, it has taken place at small community meetings led by a lone woman's voice.

It's about My Body, Dummy

My understanding of what constitutes a good population policy is simple. My right to sexual and reproductive health comes first; then, let's talk population. Although many women throughout the 20th century stated that simple message loud and clear, it took a long time for governments and the UN to listen.

The first World Conference on Population held in Bucharest in 1974 made only a passing acknowledgement of women's right to equal decision-making on population policies. It was argued that sometimes, you just have to take charge, make targets, and do everything possible to achieve them—all for the welfare of the majority of the people. Whatever human rights issues might be left pending were a small price to pay.

Subsequent failures followed, such as forced sterilization efforts and the high drop-out rates from national family planning programs. Governments were forced to rethink their strategies and became much more self-critical. India's famous campaigns to lure, pay for, and often use force to reach its population goals were a lesson for the rest of the world. Guess what? People, particularly women, do not like governments to decide how many children they should have.

The International Conference on Population and Development in 1994, which promised women more choices and freedoms than ever before, was a turning point. In 2014, the UN reinvigorated that conference plan of action, and the event was timely. Today, seven billion people inhabit the earth, and 1.8 billion are of reproductive age. This formidable challenge of balancing the carrying capacity of the earth with its human inhabitants is a feminist issue and one which we should address head on. The UN Population Fund (UNFPA) has helped keep our focus on how population trends can affect and are impacted by gender equality and women's empowerment.

• Bangladesh village women

What are the core messages we need to emphasize?

1) Girls' education is the key to a lifetime of success. Girls' education not only raises the age of marriage, but it also boosts self-esteem. Confidence and voice within the family are the magic ingredients that make adolescents more assertive, better informed about health, and better able to access the benefits of new innovations in health.

A concerted world effort has helped improve the numbers of girls attending school. More girls are enrolled in primary schools today than ever before. However, the global averages don't reflect the entrenched pockets of inequality that still affect marginalized groups, such as the disabled, pastoralists and fishing communities, ethnic minorities, indigenous girls and rural girls. For example, the illiteracy rate among indigenous women in Guatemala stands at 60 percent, more than twice the rate for men. Since these marginalized groups often manage fragile ecologies, a community's survival depends on a balance between family size and the environment.

2) We must give women the power to make decisions on their sexual and reproductive health, especially adolescents. A woman's first ecological responsibility is her body—an emotional and intelligent organic system that she should keep in balance with her environment. To maintain a balanced mental and physical well-being, she must have the right to make decisions about her own body. She must have the right to say "no" without threats to personal safety, to unsafe sex, and to population policies that violate their freedom to choose.

How can this be achieved in a short period of time? One strategic step would be to entrust men and boys with more responsibility to make it happen. This is not intellectual, wishful thinking. My grandfather broke all social convention by giving his girls university educations at a time when it was considered a privilege to boys. My father would not speak of my marriage until I had finished my PhD in my late 20s, an age which by traditional Korean standards put me on the pathway to becoming an old maid. As decision-makers in the home, men and boys can help to accelerate progress by encouraging mothers, daughters, and sisters to claim their rights and showing the way out of cultural conformity.

Although the topic of women's sexual and reproductive rights may stir controversy and debates at the UN, that is no excuse to sidestep it. The valuable recommendations of previous UN conferences should go on record as bearing the weight of global consensus. They should be displayed under bright green lights for all to see and boldly put forth as the way women view population priorities.

Frogs, Freaks and the Precautionary Principle

In the US and Canada, there have been numerous reports of frogs with too many legs and unusual eyes. Scientists suspected environmental toxins were the cause due to the frogs' soft and permeable skin, which allows chemicals to pass into their bodies. The water-land creatures are like the singing canaries that miners once used to warn them of dangerous gases. If they are in trouble, people probably are too.

School children reported the unusual occurrence, no doubt from their routine inspection of the day's catch at the local pond. In children's social circles, frogs can be traded for comic books and other useful treasures. A side benefit for children is that playing with frogs is a live science lesson.

I know this firsthand. My early experiences playing with frogs initiated an interest in environmental science. The pond near my grade school was full of wiggling baby polliwogs. My brother and I used to run knee-deep in muddy water and scoop the polliwogs into small glass jars. I mistakenly fed them a steady diet of child-preferred foods like rice to accelerate their miraculous transformations into adults. I compared the live specimens daily with pictures of frogs and anxious-

Village woman in Kashmir

ly awaited the small protrusions from the sides that were supposed to turn into webbed appendages.

My polliwogs would become hermaphroditic monsters: half fish and half frog. They were helpless, but they failed to inspire a nurturing, motherly instinct. They instead appealed to my callous scientific curiosity, the kind that motivates kids to stick pins into worms to make them squirm. Occasionally, I would chase polliwogs around the jar with my index finger to feel them move. Polliwog skin has the cold sensation of plants, and I treated my captives more like weeds than amphibians.

After a few days, I changed their water. This led to my first lesson in polliwog survival. Never put polliwogs in your own drinking water. It could kill them. The first time I put tap water into the jars, the polliwogs became listless. Then, their skins became a whitish glaze, and eventually, the poor things floated on the surface. The science class at school helped ease my conscience with a verdict of death from unknown causes. I could go to the pond and try again.

As an adult, I have pondered one question: if our household water was bad for the polliwogs, what was it doing to our health? Even without scientific proof, the logical course of action should be clear. If household water is causing polliwogs to die, then we should stay away from it. Unfortunately, as reasonable as that logic may seem, doing something about pollution is too often delayed for lack of scientific evidence.

In an era of great public confidence in scientific testimony, anything less seems unworthy. Yet, we may be paying a high price for putting off decisions that should be made now.

Many cancers, including breast cancer, are still shrouded in medical mystery and likely to remain so for many years. This has frustrated many women's health activists because governments won't commit themselves to appropriate environmental policies until the final scientific word is in. To quote a friend of mine, "Just how much longer are we going to wait? Until a whole generation of cancer victims have died while under study?"

Another issue is the many problems in environmental science and health. The WHO's 2007 report, Preventing Disease Through Health Environments noted that we don't have proper epidemiological tools to predict the impact of pollutants on our health. Many emerging risks haven't been adequately evaluated, like intensive agricultural practices, long-term chemical exposures on cancers, and electromagnetic exposures from new technologies. Hormone-mimicking pesticides, PCBs, and radiation often don't show the full range of their damage to human health until several generations have passed. To be very accurate, scientific research would have to produce much better data on women's lifestyles and their exposures to environmental hazards from birth to death—a feat that is almost impossible when research funds are limited.

Hard science is often slow to point us in the right direction. Vested interests in certain areas, such as tobacco, sometimes intentionally muddy the waters to cloud the truth. Shouldn't we use common sense as well as scientific research in creating public health policies? If canaries stop singing and frogs are born with abnormalities, I'm all for playing it safe and using the precautionary principle.

The Earth Charter Sings

There is a document that all women should care about.

It reads like a ritual: *"Rejoicing in the wonder and beauty of the Earth, we share a reverence for life and the sources of our being... Earth is our home. We are members of an interdependent community of life. Earth itself is alive."*

It is smart: *"Peace is more than the absence of violence—it is the wholeness that comes with harmonious relationship with the self, other persons, other life forms and the Earth."*

Women can find their place: *"The full participation of women at all levels of planning and management decision-making is fundamental to the achievements of equity and sustainability."*

Indigenous peoples are included: *"The culture and interests of Indigenous Peoples, including the right to control their lands and natural resources, must be respected."*

• Walking with lions in South Africa

These are passages from the Earth Charter that chairman of the 1992 Rio Earth Summit Maurice Strong and Mikhail Gorbachev introduced years ago. The Earth Charter has become the center of a global campaign among NGOs and women's groups who successfully lobbied for its adoption by the UN in 2000.

One reason it is hard to save the planet is that the values governing our decisions are wrong. A market-centric mentality is spreading like wildfire, even to the far corners of rural societies. There is a culture of profit without regard for sustainability, overconsumption, and just plain greed. Even the UN is on the wrong track when it states that human beings should be at the center of development. That anthropocentric view has led to the mistaken notion that nature can be exploited as long as human needs are fulfilled. However, our destiny is connected like a spider's web to an entire community of life. Our responsibility is to maintain balance in the entire ecosystem of planet earth.

Beatrice Schultess, a dynamic leader in the indigenous people's movement in Central America, once explained to me, "For us, the earth is a living being. More people see that now. Even a NASA scientist agreed with me that this was possible."

If what Beatrice says is true, the earth is like a breathing, growing body and the Charter is more than an international set of principles to help humanity. The Charter is intended to save all of life. It is Mother Earth's Bill of Rights.

When Phoenix Meets Dragon

Be on the lookout for a Chinese lunch special known as Phoenix and Dragon. This is a culinary combination of land and sea delights, usually chicken and shrimp. Sometimes, shrimp is replaced with squid on your plate to metaphorically represent dragons.

Symbols are partly what international politics is all about. Mind you, ingesting even symbolic dragons is no light matter. At ancient world gatherings, Chinese emperors displayed dragons on clothing, chairs, and crowns as testimony to their heavenly mandate to rule. The mere presence of the monstrous shape was supposed to attract attention—and it usually did. The phoenix was a grand symbol of the empress. The phoenix and the dragon were supposed to rule side-by-side. The phoenix's magic came from a life energy that promised rebirth out of the ruins of her own ashes. She was the force of change that moved heaven and earth, and her reign created a balance of power.

On many public occasions, such as the High Level Political Forum or UN Security Council meetings, world leaders continue to uphold the ancient dragon tradition. They charge through waves of glo-

At the Global Gender Constituency Alliance climate change booth (2018)

bal despair, hoping to fire up attention to the environment crisis. Of course, most of this dragon stuff is symbolic, but it comes with the job. At the UN Framework Convention on Climate Change (UNFCCC) meetings, heads of state should represent more than ideas and cannot afford to be mere eloquent speakers. The global climate emergency requires that leaders inspire action for change.

So where is the phoenix? Where is the spirit of renewal we need for negotiations on the environment to be a success? These days, it is found lingering among indigenous peoples and other less stately folk, where it feels much more at home. Women's organizations and civil society representatives help make up a global environment movement from the grassroots level and upward. This movement is our only chance for reviving a spirit of hope that could make governments bring international environment agreements back to life.

There is great wisdom in the ancient Chinese belief that positive influences arise from a balance between different kinds of power. We need both the spirit and agitation from local activists along with the approval and policies from governments. Women and NGOs will undoubtedly work long hours to lobby, exchange views, reach consensus, and draft amendments to a UN document. They will raise their voices in protest over the lack of equal representation on delegations and attempts to sideline their issues.

That kind of counterculture is just what is needed to balance the huffing and puffing that often surrounds inter-governmental debates. The environment and women's movement must promote a synergy with governments that brings opposite together, like the phoenix and the dragon.

(And you thought I was just talking about lunch…)

Prevention Is the Best Medicine

Any mother will tell you that when a child stops eating or has severe diarrhea, it is time to take precautionary measures. We can never be sure if the symptoms are signaling an onset of a cold, the flu, or possibly more serious diseases like malaria. However, the rules of common sense apply. Most parents use generic methods to ease the symptoms long before doctors intervene. We are survivors by nature, and as a rule, we don't like to take chances when it comes to our family's health.

The same survival techniques should apply to climate change. Rather than draw upon principles of international law that require a direct causal link between the activity and damage shown, we need to apply precautionary principles more boldly. We are all aware that the long-term effects of global warming on our health, food supplies and human settlements may not be evident to the average citizen until it is too late, but the scientific evidence is clear that human activity contributes to global warming. There are side effects we may not anticipate that could imperil our ability to survive as a human species. We would need the strength of the Hindu goddess, Durga, with her many

• At the climate change meetings, American mayors pledge support

fingers on thousands of hot spots worldwide and over millions of years to undo the damage being done today.

At various international gatherings such as the UN meetings on climate change, women leaders have called for action on global warming. Also, the Beijing Platform for Action (BPfA), a blueprint for gender equality, states, "The continuing environmental degradation that affects all human lives has often a more direct impact on women. Women's health and their livelihood are threatened by pollution and toxic wastes, large-scale deforestation, desertification, drought and depletion of the soil and of coastal and marine resources, with a rising incidence of environmentally related health problems and even death reported among women and girls. Those most affected are rural and indigenous women, whose livelihood and daily subsistence depends directly on sustainable ecosystems."

The BPfA also notes that women remain largely excluded from policy formulation on natural resources and environmental management. Women's experience and skills are also often marginalized in policy-making and decision-making bodies. Yet, women can have a powerful role in influencing sustainable consumption patterns and environmental management at the local level.

The global consensus on solutions still stands true. Governments agreed in the BPfA to the incorporation of a global perspective in the design, approval, and execution of projects funded under the Global Environment Facility. Governments should also establish strategies and mechanisms to make sure more women become active decision-makers, environment professionals and scientist, especially those at the grassroots level. This isn't just about modern science. The Platform also advocates that governments integrate rural women's traditional knowledge and practices of sustainable resource use and management.

The era of timid, cautious steps has passed. The earth's temperature is already rising near the tipping point. Now is the moment for bold, preventive action. Time is running out.

Let's Change Consumer Behavior—You First

According to some experts, we are already consuming natural resources at levels that are 30 percent above renewable. Part of the solution to this is reducing wasteful, but for many people, that remains an ideal. The prevailing attitude seems to be "Let's do it. You go first." The problem here is how to get the majority of the world's busy, working population to do its part. While I certainly support conservation efforts, I am pessimistic that changing mindsets or public campaigns are enough to change behavior. To succeed, we need to work from the other side of the equation. We need to rethink what is being produced as well as consumed.

As we search for new ideas, like withdrawing subsidies for fossil fuels and taxing air travel, we could pay more attention to old-fashioned, traditional practices that accomplish similar ends. This is particularly important in developing countries, where ecologically-appropriate products and livelihoods are rapidly being discarded, disposed, and replaced by consumer cultures. Women's experiences, which are often intermingled with traditional technologies, are particularly relevant.

Take the simple example of women's clothing. My Burmese sarong is two yards of cloth that can be wrapped and fitted at the waist whether I've overeaten or slimmed. My mother's Korean skirt that she wore when she was 16 years old still fits more than 65 years later. We can add these items to a list of everlasting garments: the Indian saree, Senegalese robes, even a revived Roman toga for men. None of these are likely to be discarded because they are designed to fit for a lifetime.

Consider knitting. In a French village, I learned that women knit endlessly for an economic reason. The beauty of wool twine is that it becomes a sweater, skirt, or pants for any child. Then, in the magical hands of the maker, it can be unraveled and remade into an adult's shawl. Similarly, quilt-making uses odd pieces of cloth and recycles the leftover contents of closets into essential bed linens. In rural Bangladesh, blankets are often made entirely out of worn-out sarees carefully hand-stitched in layers for warmth.

Rural communities in many countries provide other excellent examples of recycling systems that help reduce consumption. Service providers repair broken appliances, computers, and farm tools, partly because they are forced to use their own ingenuity and partly because they have spare parts. Most markets have special days for trading goods needed to repair radios, used furniture, and almost anything sold elsewhere in the stalls.

What if governments supported micro-enterprise loans in the service sector so that women could own businesses recycling products? If service charges rise, government subsidies could be applied to support the service sector, and consumers would find it cheaper to repair goods than throw them away. Women already have many of the skills needed to use traditional technology and products. They need a chance to combine these skills with the new. The "You first" attitude could become "Me first", and that could make all the difference.

Priming the Pumps in the Maldives

In the crystal-clear waters of Indian Ocean, the 1,200 islands of the Maldives sit like pristine stars in a constellation. Their white sands and coral reefs show off a natural ecological glow that attracts tourists from around the world. Although most citizens on these islands barely make a living, many consider their country as paradise on earth.

However, they also know they are in a fight of their lives to keep the islands pristine. A fragile ecological balance exists between the sea, plant life, and thin freshwater lenses just below the islands' surfaces. The capital Malé is an example of a future city Maldivians need. Nearly one-fourth of the country's population has settled on barely 450 acres of land over a thin water table. The freshwater supply is disappearing as fast as cool coconut juice on a hot day.

In the late 1980s, the women's unit of the Maldives government applied for a women and water project to the World Health Organization (WHO) Regional Office in New Delhi. The proposal involved a national meeting of women's groups to review progress since the last UN international conference on women and to discuss emerging issues like freshwater supply and health. The proposal was unusual because its list of essential supplies didn't include educational materials, water pumps, or medical supplies. Instead, its budget was a simple one-line item to pay for boats and fuel.

"I don't understand this proposal," my skeptical WHO colleague asked. "What do boats and fuel have to do with women's health?" Nevertheless, some of us thought that it had merit, partly because women in the Maldives were known to be well-organized and effective.

"How much do they want?" I asked.

"About $10,000" a WHO advisor answered. She continued to object to the project, noting that it was a small amount compared to huge medical projects but still seemed like a lot of money to burn up on gas. Since I was soon to visit the Maldives, the Women and Health Advisory group decided that I should investigate.

When I arrived in the Maldives, I was surprised to see that many stereotypes about women in Muslim cultures didn't apply. The local women took their religious values seriously, seizing on every possible occasion to evoke Allah's good name and benevolence. None of the women I met believed that Mohammed taught discrimination against women. The divorce rate was high, and men could easily separate from their wives. However, women were also inclined to leave husbands whom they no longer found suitable and take up with another. Women were everywhere in public—selling in markets, teaching in schools, and running small cafes. They were the main workforce in small industries, like mat and rope making and handicrafts. They also held top ranking government posts in the Ministry of Health and Planning.

The women's groups explained that their biggest problem with their water project was coordinating logistics. The Maldives' farthest islands were days away by local Dhoani boat. Members could reduce costs for their national meeting by staying with relatives, but the expensive speedboats and seaplanes used mostly for foreign tourists were out of the question. The women were willing to settle for slower, cheaper transport if only the WHO would agree to pay.

When I returned to New Delhi, I briefed the Women and Health Advisory group about the women's dilemma and the importance of transportation between the islands. The regional director quickly approved funding the project from his special account. The grant launched a great success. The women leaders had their meeting, strengthened their networks, planned new projects, and carried out public health education activities immediately.

The lesson learned is simple. It is not enough to just give civil society and women's groups a role in water development. The money sometimes has to go where the local leaders need it most, even if the requests seem highly unconventional. For the women of the Maldives, a small amount to run their boats was just what they need to fuel a national mobilization for environmental health.

Lessons from a Korean Village about Trees

One winter night in a remote Korean village, I learned how a sacred tree could bridge the divide between human beings and nature. Located deep in the woods and up a rocky pathway, a tall pine tree stood out in the full moon's light. Its unwieldy roots had dug deep into the rocky soil, its soaring branches lifted like a skirt in the wind. It didn't take much imagination to see the spirits floating around its trunk and into the forests.

This was no ordinary tree. During World War II, villagers took up arms to protect it from being cut down by Japanese soldiers. Villagers revered this tree because the mountain spirit lived in it. If they pleased the tree spirit, they said that the whole village would prosper, and many children would come for generations. The local officials held an annual festival influenced by Confucianism, during which villagers made offerings with candles, incense, rice cakes, and fruits. Bundled up in their warmest clothing, the men carried heavy loads of foods and offerings to conduct the ceremonies before midnight.

My greatest disappointment was that I was not allowed to watch the ritual. According to the village headman, no woman had ever seen

• Anthropology research in Korean village

it, so I decided to follow tradition. Resigned to staying behind, I joined a group making rice cakes after dinner by candlelight. We had our own party with delicious food and warm drinks. When I asked if they felt that they were being discriminated against for not being able to join the men, the women laughed.

"It is so cold outside," one woman explained, "and the men have to carry everything up the steep mountain trail. We are much more comfortable here." Upon hearing this, I changed my gender analysis of the situation. These women had outsmarted the men and found a way getting the rituals done by someone else.

Since then, I have learned that many rural communities and indigenous peoples hold fast to such naturalistic beliefs. Although farmers may drive tractors and wear polyester jackets, their traditional spiritual lives often survive in their subconscious. In Burma, Indonesia, Senegal and Brazil, many villagers believe that the destiny of human beings is closely connected to a web of life that includes animals, trees, rivers, and mountains. Yet these beliefs are often ridiculed, even persecuted, as superstitious and backward.

Delegates who gather at the UN climate change negotiations should take a second look at the contributions rural cultures have made to preserve the environment for centuries. Western civilization did not invent environmental ethics. Traditional cultures and indigenous peoples around the world have preserved the environment for centuries and are committed to values that can help save our planet.

The Law of Evolutionary Potential

The Law of Evolutionary Potential is a theory that most serious anthropologists consider to be defunct, unscientific, and inaccurate. Yet, time and again, this Law seems to explain anomalies about how science and technology fit with development.

According to the late anthropologist Leslie White, the originator of this theory, societies that are considered less developed on the evolutionary ladder have the greatest potential to adapt successfully when new technologies are introduced. Of course, Wright was wrong to think of evolution as a unilinear, upward process. Nor is there some abstract law that decides the direction of development. It takes real people, smart politicians, and innovation to make progress towards sustainable development work.

However, when those things are in place, poor countries that seemed destined to remain decades behind race towards solar and other sustainable energy; they suddenly look like they might become front-runners. When you start from a clean slate, why shouldn't all countries leap frog into the future?

An interesting example is the Grameen Telecom Village Phone

Starting with pure nature — rainbows at Victoria Falls

initiative that has helped village women in Bangladesh use mobile technology. Women's groups used microcredit from the Grameen Bank to buy digital GSM cellular phones, then sold the phone calls and services to others without having to leave their homes. Many have even begun to use solar charging stations. Thanks to cellular technology, Bangladesh's maternal and child health mobile registration system can boast some of the world's most comprehensive coverage.

The leapfrogging isn't necessarily limited to science and technology. Social development can also be adapted on a wider scale with a speed unknown in industrialized countries. There are emerging democracies that have moved from bottom to near the top on the gender scale of indicators, despite relatively low per capita incomes and other political and economic challenges. For example, the South African constitution requires gender equity in political representation, a provision that is the envy of women in many European countries. The South African government is also a world leader in public health legislation. While some countries retreated from bans on tobacco advertisements, South Africa already has such laws in place.

Viewing the world from the bottom rung of the evolutionary ladder may not be such a disadvantage after all. The trick seems to be making sure you study the mistakes of those who have gone before you. It takes financing research, strong support for education, and leaders willing to make the big leap forward. It would be romantic to believe that all poor countries might appear like Venus, full-grown as an energy superpower from the south. However, technological development starting from scratch can have its advantages because you don't have to disassemble old institutions or hardware. Poor countries, especially those with smart political leadership, may just show the world a few new tricks, and in one form or another, the Law of Evolutionary Potential is alive and well.

Uncommon Ground

One bright spring day in New Delhi, I looked down from my terrace to see the square patch of public land called The Commons transformed. In the past, these grounds were so barren that only retired cows visited them. However, there was a glorious garden of pink roses, white snapdragons, and marigolds. Throughout the day, visitors paced around its circular paths, endlessly inspecting the floral details. It didn't matter if you were rich or poor, young or old. If you could pull open its squeaky iron gate, a garden of Indian delights was yours.

This ecological wonder became a friendly meeting place of the neighborhood. Maybe even a few romances bloomed that year. The contribution of this garden to our social life was so amazing that I became very curious about its history. Some neighbors said that a local politician personally paid for the project, so he could get his picture in the newspapers. Others suspected that the land had been illegally sold to a private developer who restored grounds to increase the value of his own nearby property. The truth was continually rewoven into an urban folklore that blamed local woes on the bureaucracy's century-old corruption, so I never got a straight story.

The cynicism around how governments manage public projects sounded very familiar. I have spoken with women all over the world who have suffered from mismanaged public services. There is an endless list of these mismanaged services: water and sanitation programs that started well but deteriorated into a landscape of dry wells and broken water pumps, public hospitals with long waits and shortages of medical supplies, housing projects that collapsed due to mismanagement and corruption.

Women have long been among the primary advocates of a stronger role for government. The women's movement was historically united in its protest against structural adjustment policies that led to the privatization of public works. In Asia, Latin America, and Africa, women have demanded that governments withdraw from across-the-board giveaways to private enterprises because they undercut support for families. In Eastern Europe, women have called for stronger government leadership to offset the decline in free daycare and subsidized housing.

Time and again, we are told that governments must retreat from public enterprises due to financial crises. However, I suspect that the origins of the problems go much deeper and certainly much farther back than a cash shortage. Many governments are acting like severely depressed patients who are unable to act despite clear goals and ambitious plans. They are paralyzed by past failures and afraid to do any more damage, so they avoid taking risks and allow others to fail for them. As a result, the private sector gets the praise for any successes when they do occur, and this reinforces misgivings about government undertakings.

Public officials should be reminded that thousands of private-sector ventures fail daily. The equation is simple: progress requires risk. Why not dismantle government and let the free market decide? The bare truth is that no pure market mechanism would ever have built New York City's Central Park. Governments must resume their responsibility as guardians of national and global commons. Otherwise, we may lose precious ground to a wilderness of laissez-faire enterprises.

Chapter 5

Claiming the Right to Health

"My heart can't be cured because I'm too poor to pay my son's school tuition—and that is breaking my heart."

_ Korean village woman

Introduction

How can you spot a woman health activist in a crowd? She has a nagging cough, and there are dark circles under her eyes from a lack of sleep. Her feet drag as she limps into a UN meeting on women's health. For a feminist with a cause, poor health can be an unwelcome but persistent companion that reminds her that there is a price to pay for activism at the UN. During the COVID-19 pandemic, women at the frontlines and in the home often pay a high price for their own well-being.

None of this should dissuade women from joining the political fray. If we want to accomplish anything, we must have sound bodies and minds to be successful. Yet too often, we put our own health in jeopardy, and that is a mistake. Complete well-being—mental, physical and social—is the foundation for personal, economic, and political success.

Women have a very steep mountain to climb as health activists. Here are some of the major challenges that women are facing:

- The World Health Organization reports that female genital mu-

tilation, which increases the chances of poor physical and mental health in later years, affects three million girls every year.
- Although maternal mortality has steadily declined in the past decade, mothers who suffer the most are without access to universal healthcare and face discrimination based on ethnicity, race, geography, and/or religion.
- Teenage girls are exposed prematurely to sexually transmitted diseases, unsafe motherhood, and abortions. They are particularly affected by iron-deficiency anemia.
- Violence against women results in physical and mental illnesses that often go untreated. In the United States, a woman is assaulted every fifteen seconds. Refugee women experience mental trauma when they are raped or forced to have children.
- Older women who are heads of household suffer from poor nutrition, lack of health services, and disability related to lifelong deprivation and poverty.

What has governments done to protect the health of women and girls? Women's health was securely established at the UN as a human right. The definition of women's health included the highly controversial issue of women's right to sexual and reproductive health. The Beijing Platform for Action states: "The human rights of women include their right to have control over and decide freely and responsibly on matters related to their sexuality, including sexual and reproductive health, free of coercion, discrimination and violence." These are important thoughts. For the first time in intergovernmental negotiations, the right to decide what one does with one's own body and sexuality was understood as a human right that deserved protection by the state.

Women's health is also increasingly recognized as more than a purely medical issue. As the Sustainable Development Goals assert, women's health is dependent on the progress of other areas of social development, such as legal equality, economic development, and per-

• WHO helps Shanghai schools learn healthy lifestyles (2017)

sonal security. Better access to quality health services is an absolute prerequisite for the good health of women and girls. To help achieve this, improvements in girls' education, women's economic status and the environment are essential. For example, there is a correlation between women's improved education and lowered infant mortality rates. Oftentimes, the more education a woman receives, the better paying her job is and the more say she has about how to use her income. All of these benefits are better resources to keep her healthy.

Above all, women leaders, male government officials, and youth groups are starting to become active in the health realm rather than depending solely on medical specialists to make plans. The responsibility for women's health should not be left to a handful of medical elites. Most developing countries—and even industrialized ones—

view self-care and traditional medicine as important as allopathic medicine.

It is almost a cliché now that women's leadership is a human resource that can help sustainable economic development achieve its goals. However, the truth is that women's health has to come first. To strengthen the health of others, the women's movement needs to protect one of its most prized possession: the well-being of its leaders. The next time we feel like the world is about to cave in and are too exhausted to hold it up, just remember that we are only supposed to hold up half the sky. There is no shame in asking men to hold up the other half.

Discrimination Even before Birth

A village woman from Tamil Nadu, India, packed her bag and checked to make sure that she had enough money to pay the doctor. She would take the bus to a faraway city clinic for an amniocentesis test. She had become pregnant for the third time, and her husband's family told her that she must have a boy. She prayed to the gods, took herbal baths, and did almost everything the old women told her to do—all without success. If the test showed that she was having a girl, she would have an abortion at the risk of her own health. The family simply couldn't afford to have any more daughters. More girls meant more dowries.

I repeat this story as often as I can because it highlights how abuses of medical technology can perpetuate gender discrimination even before birth. This happens all too often in countries where amniocentesis is used for sex selection.

Technology itself is likely not the source of the problem. The problem is the varied ways that both clients and practitioners use technology. When I had an amniocentesis in a New York hospital, it provided very useful information. Amniocentesis samples amniotic fluid in

A child is precious

order to detect genetic problems in high-risk pregnancies. In my case, doctors confirmed that the fetus was not likely to develop a crippling birth defect such as spina bifida. That was very reassuring news.

Accounts abound about the questionable use of this important medical procedure, but few efforts by governments have worked successfully. Raising awareness around this topic is a useful first step, but it probably is not enough. We must address the root of the problem: the socioeconomic complexities of marriage. Women may want daughters, but their personal preference may have to take a back seat in favor of their family's welfare. People are concerned about expensive dowries. Daughters may leave forever and take the family's wealth with them. On the other hand, inheritance laws mean that boys are more likely to live at home after marriage and provide social security to parents in their old age. Such arguments could eventually shake the determination of the most caring parents.

Fortunately, for Indian women, the national government has tried to change health policies to avoid this abuse. Non-governmental organizations have effectively taken up issues like amniocentesis with admirable respect for women who are most affected. Giving a voice to the women who are directly affected must be the starting point of reforms—not just in the abuse of amniocentesis, but for all social and economic policies. Their choices are the ones that really can make a difference.

When Boys Will Not Be Boys

The visit to the Tunisian mobile health clinic took us out of the city, past the Roman viaduct and toward the mountain villages. Tunis disappeared behind us on a dusty winding upward road. Sparse settlements dotted the slopes, and draft animals wandered along the road. I spotted a girl on a donkey heading our way to the edge of the mountain village. Her water pails were slung on the donkey's back. I thought, 'That's progress. Girls often have to walk while the boys get the rides.'

Crowds of Berber women, some wearing beautiful earrings and long skirts, bustled around a white truck, the mobile unit. Children and some men sat nearby, watching us pull up. I was impressed to see the health clinic. Modern, spotlessly clean, and well equipped, the clinic was hard evidence that the government was serious about making contraceptives and reproductive health services accessible to everyone, even remote tribes.

On this visit, I was particularly interested in the family planning policy and its emphasis on reaching men and boys. According to the program director, doctors had been much more successful in their efforts by orienting reproductive health services to both men and women. This was known as a couple's approach.

I wanted to hear more from the men. I heard the inside story from the clinic's physician. He was a young man who had left all of the trappings of a highly specialized career to complete a round of service to rural areas. When he talked about health services for men, he explained that this clinic wanted to start education efforts early reaching out to boys. However, that was one of the most difficult parts of his assignment. He established friendly relationships with girls, as they came in with their mothers since they were young and could count on seeing them as patients when they reached puberty.

However, boys were different. They may tag along with their mothers as children. Yet, when they grew up, they shied away from his health center. He initially thought that boys had no one to mentor them in the ways of life and did not confident in adult male family members. As a result, they experienced the mysteries of changes in their bodies' functions and appearances on their own or with their peers. The brave behavior stereotypically associated with boys failed when it came to mustering up the courage to walk into a reproductive health center. Few boys, if any, ever showed up. Yet, they suffered from many disorders, including urinary tract infections and occasionally sexually transmitted diseases.

In most countries, the epidemiology of boys' sexual and reproductive health problems is a mystery to health planners. The United Nations Population Fund, which has championed women's sexual and reproductive health and rights, is also a strong advocate of the same rights for men and boys. It recognizes that cultural traditions can have gender-specific effectives, often negative, on boy's rights and freedoms.

Boys, like girls, can grow up hidden behind a veil of social taboos. Even industrialized countries that pride themselves on modern approaches to youth problems have only begun to acknowledge that the health data on adolescent boys is dismal. With drugs, alcoholism, and teenage pregnancy at the top on the list of health priorities, boys' sexual and reproductive health has fallen by the wayside, only to be picked up again when it's too late.

Let's remember that the availability of doctors doesn't automatically mean that boys will consult them. A starting point for this issue would be counseling men who attend family planning clinics to learn more about their sons' needs and advise health administrators on how to best adapt services. Progress has to start with an admission of ignorance. We cannot assume that backward traditions affect only girls. Sometimes, boys are also the losers.

A Dog's Life

If you love dogs, you would be interested to know that tourists think of Geneva as one of the world's most dog-friendly cities. This is not a trivial honor. In France and Switzerland, where dogs are pampered like children, a municipality's attitude towards dogs can be considered a measure of its moral fiber.

For some foreigners, Geneva appears to be a canine utopia where dogs are guaranteed first-class access to restaurants and public parks. Most owners can provide their loyal pets with basic needs, like housing with the amenities of warm beds and treats.

Genevans boast about their humane treatment of animals, but is their claim justified? I thought so until my recent visit to the city. On the surface, things looked pretty good. Geneva offers better habitats for dogs than cities like Beirut or Bangkok. In those cities, a dog's life is a wild and dangerous existence. There is such disdain for dogs in the Islamic tradition that a Muslim's worst insult would include comparisons to dogs in a string of profanities. In Bangkok, polluted waters and toxic dumps afflict many animals, so they have chronic skin sores. Although Beijing and Seoul may offer strict ordinances to control

Rick and me with Cooper and Sophie

pollution, I wouldn't want to be a dog in either metropolis. Dogs are reportedly kidnapped, caged, fattened, then served up as dog soup.

On the other hand, Genevans put dogs in front of the plate, not on it. At the most elegant lakeside restaurants, dogs happily sniff the cordon bleu aromas while lingering under the tables. When dining at a famous bistro, I spied a large gold retriever strategically positioned among fellow beef lovers. Between pats on the head and admiring greetings from the waiters, she licked her paws and eyed her midnight snack. Swiss pets return the favor of their public privileges with characteristic national civility. I never saw a dog beg at another client's table. Few things in Switzerland are enigmatic, but how pets abide by a code of good behavior is a true mystery.

Life for dogs is equally congenial at the Geneva Botanical Gardens. On a sunny spring Sunday, owners treat dogs to long walks along the lake. One day, I spotted a dachshund running about without his leash. No one seemed to think that he was overstepping his boundaries when he ran off to greet other dogs. All pets without leashes were presumed to belong to someone, and I never saw a homeless dog wandering about. The owner would call out occasionally, and the dog would dutifully rejoin the family walk. (I observed that Swiss children behaved in a similar fashion.)

My opinion of Genevans was increasingly favorable, and I was ready to give Geneva the Légion d'honneur medal for canine treatment when my Zimbabwean friend Rudo Mungwashu objected. She pointed out that since a large number of Swiss people are smokers, those with pets must subject them constantly to secondhand smoke. Dogs often frequent smoky bars and restaurants, so pregnant dogs and puppies must be also affected.

I had seen alarming evidence about secondhand smoke for humans. It increases children's risk of middle ear infections, respiratory diseases, and asthma, and causes heart and lung diseases in women. The WHO's report on Gender, Women and Tobacco (WHO, 1998) states that prolonged exposure to secondhand smoke can cause lung cancer and that women who live with partners who smoke may also be at great risk for heart disease. All of this is bad news for pregnant women, children, and pets who live with smokers.

However, I had never seen any statistics on the impact of secondhand smoke on dogs. Animals were nonexistent on national health statistics, and exposure to secondhand smoke was an unknown—but possible—cause of canine death. Rudo had a point. As a true dog lover, I had to disqualify Geneva as a dog's heaven.

Rural Women as 'Medical Women'

One of my first UNICEF assignments was in Burma (now Myanmar), where I evaluated the training of traditional birth attendants (TBAs). In the early 1980s, Dr. Tin Tin Hmun, former director of maternal and child health for the Ministry of Health, was experimenting with blending traditional values and practices with modern medicine. When I arrived at a village health center, a dozen or so elderly women were hovering around a paper cutout that was shaped like a woman's womb. Beside this prop was a cloth doll. One of the women put her lips to the doll's lips and started mouth-to-mouth resuscitation.

Dr. Hmun explained that this new skill was helping to save newborn lives and that TBAs were very willing to learn new techniques. She was able to work with her community because she also respected older beliefs. None of the older women could read or write, but Dr. Hmun believed that they had extraordinary skills. Some of their techniques may have come from vast experience. We estimated that collectively in their lifetimes, the TBAs had delivered about five thousand babies. The role of these elderly women extended beyond

• Burmese traditional birth attendants

delivery; they were also advisors for prenatal and postnatal care and provided psycho-social support for mothers through the stressful post-partum period.

I asked one TBA what she used to do before she learned about reviving babies the modern way. "We used to take the placenta over to an open fire and fry it", she explained. When I asked if she thought that a fried placenta really helped newborns, she answered that she wasn't sure, but it always encouraged mothers when someone was doing something.

Now that a better and proven method was known, the TBA said that everyone agreed to do mouth-to-mouth resuscitation instead. On the other hand, there was one practice they wouldn't give up: cutting the umbilical cord over a coin with a sharp piece of bamboo. "That brings good fortune," said a TBA. However, to limit possible infections, Dr. Hmun instructed TBAs to sterilize the coin and bamboo along with cloths and other utensils.

In other countries, I have found rural women as traditional healers, herbalists, specialists of ancestral spiritual traditions, and traditional birth attendants. Even today, this elite corps of rural village women can be found practicing oftentimes in cities. For that reason, I suggest that these rural village women are medical women in the broadest sense whose greatest asset often cannot be matched by modern doctors. These women are well-versed in traditional health culture and are locally available.

We have to add the local women to the ranks of rural women healthcare providers. Local women extend to mothers, mothers-in-law, and grandmothers. For example, in Korean villages, mothers-in-law are TBAs and expected to be called upon to bring a new life into this world. Mothers-in-laws in rural areas conduct rituals to ensure that ancestors came to help new parents and gave advice to young mothers about nutrition, such as avoiding certain foods like hot, spicy soups. In the post-partum period, these women also make sure that families observed the proper seclusion period, so "cold winds" would not enter a mother's womb and make her sick.

Why do we still need to pay attention to rural women as part of the healthcare delivery system? The conventional argument is still valid: women are the key decision-makers in family health. The majority of health decisions are made at this level. Rural women's knowledge must be employed to ensure food security, good child nutrition, family use of water and sanitation, and environmental management. Modern medical practitioners must learn to speak in terms that rural women understand. If not, modern medicine will further lose the knowledge from rural women's longstanding concepts of illness.

Poor women in cities and villages are the largest corps of unpaid, unappreciated, and unacknowledged healthcare providers. They must be recognized as a resource on socioeconomic development. If traditional birth attendants and other local healers can improve their skills and become successfully integrated into Maternal and Child Health programs, imagine how much richer our medical knowledge would be.

The Victims—It's Time to Stop Blaming Them for AIDS

In the off-hours of Bangkok's busy nightlife, massage parlor workers take off their number badges and step out of their fish tank-like windows where they sit waiting for customers to choose them. Dancers unhook themselves from ropes that support their athletic prances. They gather around steaming cups of tea and catch up on the latest television soap operas. While these daily routines restore a mood of normalcy to the intense, burned-out life of these young women, everyone is aware that nothing about this life is normal. Many of them must provide sexual services, as well as entertainment and massages. Since the AIDS epidemic hit Thailand in the 1980s, sex work has become a game of hide-and-seek with death.

Non-governmental organizations, government programs, and women's groups have made sure that AIDS awareness has reached the entertainment business. Public health clinics have been set up in the midst of the neon-lit glimmer of the infamous Patpong tourist district. The clinics show videos for health education programs nonstop for patients in the waiting rooms. Women's groups also established outposts in the same area. Activists are determined to raise the gender bias issues. They have highlighted the plight of child prostitutes, the near slave-like conditions of massage parlors, and the sexist bias of health programs. Their mission is urgent.

I ventured into Patpong with a government health worker. An elderly Chinese couple that owned the bar greeted us with a bow and told us that they hoped the AIDS scare was just a rumor. We told them that the situation was very critical and that their cooperation would be an important contribution to remedy the problem.

As the time approached for the health education session to begin, the bar girls came downstairs from their quarters. I quickly surveyed that their faces that were freshly scrubbed and had no makeup. Some looked like they were in their teens, although they probably had false identification cards. They chattered on like Bangkok swallows, pushing close to each other as they settled into the bar booths.

When the NGO nurse arrived, the noise subsided into an obedient silence, and the bar girls sat up attentively like students starting the day with their teacher. The lights dimmed, and the slide show began with hopeful musical messages about how sexually transmitted diseases are treatable and where to go for help. A somber tone quickly replaced the gay mood. The photos were unusually explicit, showing skin sores and the cancer-eaten flesh of AIDS patients. Some bar girls looked away. Everyone was pretty frightened by the end of the slide show.

The young women were very receptive to the main message of the day to use condoms. Heads bobbed in agreement. When the lights came up, the nurse took out her packets of condoms and did a perfect finger demonstration of how they slip on. Then, she offered one packet to each girl. One by one, they knelt in front of the nurse who assumed an air of a merciful angel. The bar girls received their gifts with their eyes to the ground and hands folded in respect.

Then, one young woman dared to ask, "How can we get men to wear these condoms? Do you have any suggestions?"

"You must tell men that they might get AIDS or other diseases if

• Thai sex education in Bangkok red light district (1985)

they don't," the nurse answered with an authoritative voice. That comment ended the friendly session, and everyone said farewell.

The leader of the group of girls, known as the "men's favorite," sat down with me and my translator. She assured me that the bar girls took these education messages seriously and were grateful that NGOs wanted to help. The only problem was that they could not make men put on condoms. They couldn't explain this to the nurse and had learned to be realistic about the tourism business.

"If we tell men that they will get AIDS, they won't come back, and we will lose our jobs," she said.

I compared this situation with those of some European countries where sex workers were mostly mature, assertive adults capable of organizing themselves into semi-unions. However, these bar girls had barely crossed the threshold from childhood to womanhood. From their perspective, the grand vision of the feminist movement about empowerment for young women seemed out of reach. In the eyes of Thai society, prostitutes are so-called "bad girls" who lived in a world of drugs and crime that was largely hidden from sight.

Nevertheless, a few women's groups are working to shed light on an underground world of crime, kidnapping, and rape. Their actions are beginning to attract public attention. Prostitution is officially illegal, but enforcing the law is another matter. There are networks of sex slave traders who have cast their nets across Thailand's hill tribes and poorer northern regions to entrap more girls. Some of the victims are as young as ten years old. The age slips lower as the AIDS epidemic progresses and the demand for virgins increases.

Feminists report the there are two underlying causes of prostitution: poverty and efficient sex trafficking organizations. Impoverished rural parents sell their daughters under the guise of paying a job broker as low as $200 to help girls find a job in a city. However, the broker is actually trafficking girls from rural villages to cities. Under changing hands many times, the victims may find themselves in tearooms as child prostitutes. Later, they are moved into the bars and massage parlors to service international tourists and businessmen.

Clients from Germany, France, and England have been lured by ads. One ad was posted by a Swiss travel group: "Slim, sun-burnt and sweet, [Thai prostitutes] love the white man in an erotic and devoted way. They are masters of the art of making love by nature, an art that we Europeans do not know." Japanese, Chinese, Thai, and Arab businesses also entertain at establishments where customers can step into rooms in the back for a little "special treatment."

The tragedy of prostitution in many countries, such as the Philippines, Korea and Indonesia, is that the victims have often been blamed for the AIDS epidemic. Sex workers are portrayed as the new Typhoid Marys who carry the HIV virus. Health campaigns often focus exclusively on the health education, control, and surveillance of prostitutes, rather than that of their male clients. If this was not enough, improved surveillance among prostitutes has meant that those who contract the virus lose their jobs without health insurance or job compensation to cushion the financial blow.

It is time to stop blaming the victims. Women activists have called for more legal action and health education directed at the organizers of sex trafficking and male clients. More concerted action is needed because the HIV/AIDS epidemic kills the most vulnerable women and girls. More women than men have AIDS worldwide, and UNAIDS (https://www.unaids.org/en/aboutunaids) reports that HIV prevalence among female sex workers ranged from 6.1 percent in Latin America to 36.9 percent in sub-Saharan Africa.

Let me end my story with a reminder of how rural poverty lies at the heart of the matter. Several months after my Patpong visit, I traveled to a poor northeast region near the Laotian border. I met a couple on their farm who were caring for a young child. They told me that she belonged to their daughter and that she did not have a father to take care of her. Then, they told me proudly of their beautiful daughter and how she left to find work in the city at a big restaurant. I asked the name of the restaurant, since I would go back to Bangkok and might take their greetings to her. They said that they didn't know, but the job must have paid very well, since she sent money home every month.

I looked at the child and remembered the bar girls in Patpong. I told the couple that perhaps I will meet their daughter in the city, but I did not say where it might be—in a restaurant, bar, or hospital for AIDS patients.

A Gift from a Child with Leprosy

A slim boy hobbled on his lame leg to catch up with me. I turned to see a young face covered with dark lesions. The hot summer breeze lifted the smell of his tattered clothing into the air and followed him like a shadow. He had tattered bandages on his fingers that reminded me of Lazarus rising from the dead. A case of leprosy on two legs was heading toward me. I turned about and quickened my pace.

I wasn't afraid of the boy. I had just spent a week at a leprosy center in Wardha, India. I knew that a leper's casual touch never gave anyone else the disease. It took long and continual contact to transmit the disease. Then why did I instinctively turn away? I think it was the instinct to avoid any street beggar.

I thought that I'd hurry along to finish my errands. In New Delhi, if you start giving coins to a street beggar, you become surrounded by more. It was better not to get involved. My eyes spotted a taxi nearby. The boy called out in Hindi as if he had an emergency; he became more and more agitated. I worried that his keepers would beat him if he didn't bring in money, so I stopped. When he reached me, he smiled and extended his thin arm to hand me something. It was my pen that I had dropped on the ground. Before I could thank him, he went off to join the lepers' huddle against a dirt wall.

There was no medical reason this child should have had leprosy. The disease is curable. With the help of the World Health Organization, a treatment known as multidrug therapy (MDT) has reduced leprosy incidence by 85 percent. The achievement is not as well-heralded as it ought to be. If infected individuals go to a health clinic when they first notice the skin spots, they can be cured with MDT within six months. After the first dose, they are no longer infectious and can mingle in close contact with their family and friends. Early detection has probably prevented about one to two million people from becoming disabled. MDT is a miracle drug this boy should have had.

However, stigma and deformity have made access to MDT impossible. Many children do not have enough sensation in their limbs to avoid accidents that can lead to losing fingers and hands, such as burns. At the Wardha Center, founded by Mahatma Gandhi, artificial hands and legs were fashioned to help leprosy patients with their rehabilitation. With the help of education programs about the affliction in local communities, leprosy patients can marry and raise families. Their children do not inherit the disease. In some Indian areas where social awareness has been raised, leprosy patients have gotten jobs and have become productive members of their community.

Biomedical research has done its job by finding the miracle cure, but there is more work to be done. Continuing stigma prevents some doctors from specializing in leprosy, if not even learning about the disease. As a result, we have reached an impasse. MDT could help us eradicate the pockets of endemic leprosy in India, Nepal, and about 20 other countries. However, we must first decide that helping children with leprosy is a priority.

I lost the old pen. However, the boy gave me a very special gift to last a lifetime: a glimpse into a child's innocence is as pure as their beginnings. His small gesture of forgiveness for my misunderstanding showed compassion beyond his years.

When Medicine Is Not Enough

Mrs. Kim was a Korean traditional herbalist, the kind that people went to for every kind of ailment—mental, physical, social. She did not stand out among the older village women dressed in puffy, loose pants that blew around her slim legs like noisy flags when she walked. Her hands had the firm clasp of someone used to gathering heavy firewood and pulling stubborn weeds out of gardens.

Her most valuable inheritance from her late husband was the knowledge of traditional medicine that she picked up as his lifelong assistant. When I met her, she was running a grocery store slash herbal shop to support her son, who had just finished his second year at Yonsei University. Villagers turned to her sage advice on treating arthritis, the common cold, and much more. If children were doing poorly in school, Mrs. Kim offered parents words of comfort and hints on how to motivate them. When babies refused to breastfeed, she visited the family and helped sooth tensions about who was to blame. If she couldn't help patients with herbs, she made sure that they visited the local health clinic.

In brief, she was a rural social worker, physical therapist, herbalist, and psychiatrist combined. I dubbed her the village social doctor because she could cure many of the community's social ills.

However, Mrs. Kim herself was ill. She had been in and out of the hospital for treatment of serious hypertension. When I asked about her health, she threw up her arms in exasperation. She said that many doctors had prescribed medicines, but not one had been successful. When she used herbal medicines and acupuncture, the symptoms just returned. She confided in me that after many months, she finally discovered the cause of her illness: her son's school fees. Every year, a few months before his tuition was due, her condition would worsen. She would have trouble sleeping because of her worries. She also stopped paying for her own medication in order to save for her son's needs.

"That is why modern medicine can't cure me," she explained. As long as she was poor and had to support her son, she didn't think she would get better.

Too often, the relationship between poverty and health is reduced to simple solutions like building another health clinic for the poor. If Mrs. Kim is to be truly cured, she must have access to anti-poverty programs and subsidies for school fees as well as affordable medical services. When she recovered, she would have more money to invest in her son's education.

At the household level, parents' health and children's education are intimately linked, and mothers are often the ones making the connections. If we improve women's incomes and provide socioeconomic support, we will very likely raise the living standard of an entire family. At the meetings on the Sustainable Development Goals, we all must become the world's social doctors focusing on social as well as physical and mental health.

The Trials of Being a Traditional Healer

Why are most Asian babies born with a birthmark that looks like a bruise at the base of the spine? Doctors and traditional midwives have different explanations for the Mongolian spot. According to medical experts, the bluish-grey blotch is a genetic gift from the parents that will gradually fade. However, if you ask a Korean rural villager about its origins, you might get a different answer. An old woman told me that babies need a little kick to help them come into this world. Life is so hard, and they don't want to be born. A three-spirit deity of heaven, earth, and the underworld gives the baby a gentle push, leaving a tell-tale trace on the baby's back.

In real life, traditional healers, such as three-spirit grandmothers, took charge of maternal and child healthcare once the baby was born. These traditional healers were the consultants on child nutrition, illness, and post-partum recovery for the first one hundred days of the baby's life. They also performed rituals of prayer, food offers, and songs for ancestors to watch over the infant's well-being.

Traditional, rural Korea is no exception. In many countries, the largest groups of healthcare providers in rural areas are women known as traditional birth attendants (TBAs) and female traditional healers. Village women often trust their strong moral character and years of experience—qualities that they say are sometimes missing among younger, modern doctors.

For decades, UN agencies such as UNICEF and the UNFPA regarded TBAs as invaluable human resources for providing health services, including immunization, family planning, and nutrition education. Training programs across the world were highly successful in mobilizing their support to reach women and help bridge the gap between modern and traditional health systems.

"We have sterilized birthing kits," one healer explained to me, "but we also stick to our traditions, like cutting the umbilical cord on a coin so that the child will have good fortune. Doctors have taught us how to sterilize the coin and knife beforehand."

Although TBAs and women healers participate in government-sponsored programs, few health policymakers are aware of the problems that these women face when carrying out their work. These women suffer from gender bias that keep them at the bottom of a health hierarchy, much like their counterparts in modern medicine. For example, in Korea, the herbalists and acupuncturists who dominate the upper levels of the traditional medical system are mostly men, many of whom are literate and practiced in cities. Below them were shamans, fortune-tellers, three-spirit grandmothers, and traditional midwives.

Female traditional healers are poor, illiterate, and landless heads of households. Their fees are typically lower than those of male specialists, so even after years of practice, they can still barely make ends meet. It is common for them to be paid in-kind. One shaman I knew usually received bags of rice, chickens, and clothing as payment. She never complained and always accepted whatever the patients could offer because she felt that her mission in life was to serve everyone equally. However, there was never enough money to pay for many homeless friends who dropped in for a free meal or a quick loan.

Another obstacle that TBAs and women healers face is prejudice from doctors who believe these women discourage patients from using modern health services. While this has likely happened, the degree of competition is far less than one might expect. In Korea, Thailand, and Burkina Faso, I found that healers themselves often use modern medicine. For example, one traditional healer had facial cancer and was being treated in a high-tech cancer clinic. In her view, it was not a matter of modern versus traditional medicine, but rather how patients perceived their needs. Healers see themselves as helping to restore the will to live because they typically deal with patients who are discouraged by ailments requiring long-term care, like tuberculosis and cancer. They also help patients survive depression and psycho-social complications after birthing that might interfere with effective treatment by modern physicians.

Much more anthropological research is needed on how medical pluralism affects women healers and their patients. Ultimately, the losers are the poor, many of whom are women, who go back and forth from one system to another, looking for someone who will treat the whole person—mind, body, heart, and soul.

How Secondhand Smoke Disappeared from the UN

When people ask me if the UN can make a difference, I think of one positive example. At the UN headquarters in New York, air pollution once afflicted many of us attending the Commission on the Status of Women (CSW) meetings. The source wasn't noxious fumes from automobiles contaminating the indoor air. Rather, there were clouds of carcinogenic particles billowing over our heads and right under our noses in the Vienna Café. Cigarette smokers of all genders and nationalities were everywhere. If the World Health Organization had done an air pollution test, it would have clearly declared this area unfit to support life. Yet, in the 1990s, smoking was permitted in this public area.

I wasn't so upset that women and men were indulging in cigarettes. After all, the sign posted near the trash only said that smoking was discouraged, not banned. I had more selfish notions in mind. Since I had kicked the habit years ago, I was determined not to let all the smoke tempt me. As it turned out, there was no escape.

Ironically, women's health was a priority topic on that year's CSW agenda. In a nearby conference room, the NGO Committee for the

• WHO health champions Dr. Douglas Bettcher and Menno Van Hilten (2016)

CSW on Mental Health was having intense discussions about women and substance abuse. I was listening to a doctor discuss drugs in the workplace when I got a distinct whiff of cigarette smoke. It had to be coming from the vents that circulate the air throughout the building. There was no way to open a window; there weren't any. Anyone who has sat in a restaurant's no smoking section knows how that feels. Air roams freely with total disregard for any signs and into every corner of a building.

"Why doesn't the UN do something?" complained one NGO participant. "If the UN delegates don't set an example, how can they expect the rest of the world to stop smoking?"

Someone defended the UN, noting that in many buildings, including the World Health Organization headquarters, smoking was

• WHO anti-tobacco poster

banned. We were puzzled about where to submit an appeal because no one knew who was responsible for the UN house rules. Whoever it was, they might consider that building workers and food servers could easily sue for prolonged exposure to air pollution if they developed respiratory diseases.

The tobacco problem aside, everything else was going smoothly at the CSW meeting. The Convention on the Elimination of All Forms of Discrimination against Women (CEDAW) Committee completed its elaboration on Article 12 concerning women's health. It is implicitly understood that it is the duty of states to act swiftly and decisively to guarantee that women can exercise their human rights to health. These clarifications were then expressed to the CSW and discussed by a panel of experts. WHO representatives speaking for the World Health Organization Framework Convention on Tobacco Control (WHO FCTC) took a bold stand in support of the women's health movement and decried the tobacco companies' aggressive campaigns to promote smoking. Women's health was getting solid political support from all major groups, who were quickly becoming instant health experts.

We were still obliged to discuss our health priorities in the polluted environment of the UN Building. When I got home, I was reminded that there is another downside to smoking: the odor. My hair, papers, and clothing were all saturated with the smell of cigarettes. My daughter asked me suspiciously if I had been smoking. Having breathed the smoke-filled air at the UN for hours, I had to answer, "Yes."

Today, this is no longer true. Smoking was finally prohibited at UN headquarters in 2008 through a resolution of the General Assembly.

Good for Me, but Not for Thee

The historic Beijing Platform for Action stated: "The human rights of women include their right to have control over and decide freely and responsibly on matters related to their sexuality, including sexual and reproductive health, free of coercion, discrimination and violence... the ability of women to control their own fertility forms an important basis for the enjoyment of other rights."

These statements were major victories for women's human rights and empowerment, and the United States was one of the 181 governments that signed. However, the Platform's opponents quickly moved to undercut its advances. The Helms Amendment, championed by the arch-conservative Jesse Helms, stated that American foreign aid could not be used to help pay for abortion services.

From the point of view of poor village women in Bangladesh, the United States may seem guilty of a double standard. While American women won the right to abortion in *Roe V. Wade*, the Helms Amendment sent the message that the United States didn't support these same rights for others.

American foreign aid is a mere fraction of what American taxpay-

• Rural health workers (1980)

ers spend abroad and makes up less than 0.05 percent of the federal budget. Nevertheless, the US dollar carries great symbolic weight in poor countries plagued with famine and poverty. In rural Bangladesh, the impact of American policy on sexual and reproductive health is profound. One pilot-project area reported that an estimated one out of every five maternal deaths was due to complications from abortions. About 10 thousand women in Bangladesh alone meet the same fate every year.

I learned of one of these cases during a visit to a rural health clinic. A woman named Rataner was left with two children after her husband died. She remarried but later discovered that her second spouse had other wives. Four and a half months pregnant, and without means to support her children, she obtained traditional herbs from her sister-in-law and used these to abort her fetus. The bleeding did not stop, and she fainted. Although she could have gotten medical attention in a distant hospital, she was never taken there. She died a few days later.

"Our hands are tied," a project worker confided in me. "Women are dying from botched abortions, but we cannot provide the services for them. We need foreign help after all."

Unfortunately, many developing countries have no choice but to accept the conditions of those who offer support. Bangladesh's family planning program is heavily dependent on American funds. One of the poorest countries in the world, Bangladesh has only a few hospital beds for every 100,000 people. Although its population growth rates are declining, Bangladesh faces a severe shortage of doctors, nurses, and health centers.

Unexpected pregnancies are a heavy burden for impoverished families on the brink of starvation. Another mouth to feed deprives the entire family of a chance to survive. Industrialization is also creating new social problems. Most of the women in Bangladesh must rely on a mix of modern and traditional forms of fertility regulation, both of which are highly unreliable. Rural women who start with oral contraceptives and become dissatisfied with its side effects often switch to something else or take the pill intermittently. If unwanted pregnancies occur—and modern health services can't help—families turn to traditional health practitioners.

The impact of the Helms Amendment isn't limited to sexual and reproductive health. It also inhibits AIDS prevention. Condoms are supposed to help prevent HIV/AIDS infections while safeguarding against unwanted pregnancies. However, they have a high failure rate. Unless safe abortions can be available on request, clients will be reluctant to use them.

How can American feminists help? They must become better informed about American aid policies affecting the sexual and reproductive rights of women abroad. Anti-abortion policies violate international agreements on women's reproductive rights signed by the American government. A double-standard guiding American foreign aid not only hurts poor families, but also hurts the government's credibility even more.

My "Untouchable" Indian Doctor

When I was sick with hepatitis in New Delhi and faced with the possibility of being bedridden for days, I decided to find out what kind of doctors treated the lower castes and tribal peoples of India. I had heard that most modern doctors of high caste origins preferred practicing privately among the urban elites. By all traditional standards of caste purity, there was to be no symbolic or physical contact with untouchables. Even if the high-caste doctors were willing to cross caste lines, most untouchables and tribal peoples could not afford to pay their high fees.

"Biwani, I am not feeling very well and my stomach hurts. Can you ask your doctor to please come quickly?" I asked my friend's Muslim house servant.

"Yes, saab (madame in Hindi)," he answered enthusiastically. "I know a good doctor. I will go to the market and get him right away."

I wondered what kind of doctor he could find in the market. My imagination conjured up images of untrustworthy quacks sitting in stalls, waiting like hawkers selling chickens for gullible patients. Would this market be equipped with dirty syringes and leftover antibiotics? Perhaps I had taken this experiment too far.

When Biwani returned, he was smiling triumphantly. A doctor was at his side, carrying an authoritative medical bag. My hopes rose. He looked like he might be licensed after all. In fact, he looked like a dentist I used to have as a child, the only one I would let drill my teeth. I thought strange that although I knew nothing about him, his near-perfect English immediately inspired confidence in his medical qualifications. His questions were brief, and he narrowed the possibilities to one conclusion.

"You have a mild case of hepatitis," he said. "As you know, you need plenty of rest. If you are interested in some modern Ayurvedic medicine, I can recommend Liv-52. You must try to eat more lentils and rice."

I was anxious to find out how this refined, well-mannered doctor ended up treating peddlers and servants in the market rather than practicing in a hospital. He willingly told me his sad story. He was originally from a remote mountainous tribe. With the help of Christian missionaries, he was educated in the best schools and passed exams to study medicine. He completed his education, married a tribal woman, and looked forward to a happy medical career.

He quickly learned that caste differences got in the way. Few hospitals would hire him. His attempts at private practice failed as well. Hiding his tribal identity only worked for a while; eventually, someone would uncover his tribal status, and he would have to move on. Finally, he arrived at the New Delhi market where there were enough Muslims, tribal, and lower caste people who needed medical care. To his delight, foreigners like me sought his advice as well.

When he finished his story, I thought about India's shortage of doctors. In the 1990s, less than three percent of the people of the hill tribes had access to modern medicine. Only one in one hundred thousand people in the whole country was treated by physicians in hospitals. In principle, educating more doctors and nurses would have helped remedy this situation.

However, the great experiment of equality through education faces many challenges. Unfortunately, for this doctor, educational achievement was not the gateway to equal opportunity. There is one real question that remains. Who is the real loser: the doctor, or the patient?

Chapter 6

Economic Empowerment

"Your education is the only wealth you can carry with you throughout your life."

_ Dr. Song Pok-Shyn

Introduction

The World Bank has said that gender equality is good economics. Although that may be a compelling argument for a minister of finance, it implies that gender equality is important as an economic instrument. Somehow that argument does not sit well with my feminist priorities to put women's welfare first.

The economic-utility argument is not completely wrong; it is misleading. My feminist argument would rather say that gender equality is good governance because it assures equality in economic decision-making. When viewed through a human rights lens, good economic policies uphold the principles of shared benefit, inclusiveness, and sustainability—all very much a part of a gender equality approach.

The biggest challenge for many of us is to argue for a feminist perspective on macroeconomic policies. However, let's start with issues that lie close to home like gender-based violence. Violence against women and girls is an extreme form of coercion, a barrier to full economic decision-making. If the goal of development is to broaden and enhance personal freedoms, ending violence against women and girls is clearly a prerequisite for economic empowerment, rather than just achieving economic growth.

We also need to look with skepticism at fiscal consolidation and reducing government debt, which often results in cuts in social services, such as health care, daycare centers, and social protection measures. These cuts affect women the most because women are the ones most negatively affected by disasters, financial crises, and health crises. During the COVID-19 pandemic, a lack of affordable childcare forced many women to withdraw from the work force.

Finally, macroeconomic policies related to infrastructure and trade must be planned using a gender lens. For example, improved infrastructure plans, road construction, and public transportation improvements can improve women's efficiencies, particularly in developing country where they depend on animals for firewood. Women must jump into mainstream economic discussions and demand a say in financing for development.

This Is the Hand That Built

This is the hand that raised the kids
that played in the kitchen
that had the pot
that cooked the corn
that sold in the market
that fed the family
that lived in the house
that Maria built.

Look at a house from a poor woman's point of view. It is more than a shelter for sleeping and eating; it is also a woman's primary workspace. Whether this work is paid or not may change over a lifetime. When children are young, a woman may work mainly as an unpaid housekeeper. However, a shelter can also be a place where she earns her living. If she is disabled, she can do home-based jobs, such as sewing. If she is a peddler traveling around the city, she must prepare her goods at home. An older woman can set up a small store right at the front door. She can cure the sick and care for children at home.

Rural Women make pots

The list of activities seems endless. There is one thing she is not likely to do at home: retire.

One error of many governments' discussions about the home is assuming that men and women use it in the same way. Participants at UN meetings about economic development, including urban planners, academics, and scientists, often talk about a home from a male perspective: a place that you leave when you go to work. Home is considered a private space without connections to the public arena of commerce and politics. From a working woman's point of view, this private space cannot be separated from their public life.

Reproduction, production, and consumption are the three pillars of a household economy. A woman is the fourth pillar, and she must keep the others balanced to take care of the whole family. If her job requires long-distance travel, and there is no daycare facility at work, she must find alternative care for the children. In many families, daughters drop out of school to help the family survive. Women must also consider their responsibilities as consumers of goods and services. A home's location near a good school, water pumps, quality public services, and stores is as important for a family's welfare as low-cost housing.

These are some critical gender and housing issues that need to be remembered in the Sustainable Development Goals. These issues cover living conditions that many of us know exist but are not always reflected in the outcome of a UN consultation. Policy-makers are prone to apply a double standard to women and shelter issues. They do not mind bringing women into the picture when referring to personal security or family life. However, they are less inclined to listen when women declare that housing is a political matter. Women want and should have more decision-making power about housing rights, including issues related to land and other assets.

Women's rights are at stake when speaking about socioeconomic policies that create conflicts between women's multiple roles. For example, to increase women's economic participation, policies may favor foreign investments in export-oriented trade zones that attract a female work force. However, these jobs are often incompatible with women's duties at home. There are few support services for childcare in these industrial parks even if management openly approves of working mothers.

Another example of this conflict between socioeconomic policies and women's many roles is how poverty affects family planning. Poor women may have access to family planning services, but quality services do not guarantee that women have the choice to make decisions about reproduction. Women and health activists point out that in some Latin American countries, women appear to have access to a variety of family planning methods, but still undergo mass sterilization due to of poverty. They simply cannot afford to give up work days or extra money for visits to health clinics. True family planning is only possible when there are economic opportunities as well. These economic opportunities have declined for women due to the global economic crisis and higher fees for public services.

As we look to the future, I think of one important message from the International Labor Organization and the Beijing Platform for Action. To create compatibility between work and family, it is crucial to attain sustainable development. Let the women who speak from real-life situations have an equal say in how family and work fits into the bigger pictures.

Four Wishes for Economists

There was once a little girl who was supposed to write a class assignment called "My Hopes and Dreams." The problem was that she was unsure about grammar, so she carefully chose her words and wrote down each thought. Then, at the top of the first page, she wrote a note to the teacher, "I have written this essay with everything except the punctuation and capital letters. Since you are the expert, could you please fill these in? Thank you."

Only a fanciful child would suggest such a collaborative approach to writing about her own hopes and dreams. It would be hard to imagine why a smart-thinking adult would surrender control of the tools that give logic and coherence to important thoughts. Yet, in the running of our economies, this seems to happen quite frequently, and usually with questionable results.

After politicians make major policy decisions, they busy themselves with governing, leaving the real business of running the economy to the so-called experts: economists, finance ministers, and development planners. Most of these professionals are more concerned with the science of social engineering than with the ethical or ideo-

• NGO scoreboard of commitments in Beijing (1995)

logical issues of politics. There is little wonder that the hopes and dreams expressed at UN conferences often lose their meaning once the heads of state have signed the papers and gone home. The real decision-makers, otherwise the ones who ultimately write the checks, are never invited to the meetings in the first place.

If ministers of finance are to change their mission from economic development to sustainable human development, then the people who run their economies will have to become much more than economists. They will also have to be social activists who are willing to dialogue with community groups and non-governmental organizations. They will also have to become more involved in the not-so-predictable world of international diplomacy.

It would behoove to study the commitments that heads of state have made at UN conferences long ago and to take the collective ideologies expressed in them seriously. Governments might consider these four passages chosen from historic UN conferences that express important visions for humanity:

1. "We, Heads of State and Government...will create a framework for action to...[promote] democracy, human dignity, social justice, and solidarity at the national, regional and international levels, ensure tolerance, non-violence, pluralism and non-discrimination in full respect of diversity within and among societies." (Social Summit, 1995)

2. "The human rights of women and of the girl-child are an inalienable, integral and indivisible part of universal human rights...The World Conference on Human Rights...reaffirms, on the basis of equality between women and men, a woman's right to accessible and adequate health care and the widest range of family planning services..." (Vienna Declaration, Conference on Human Rights, 1993)

3. "Peoples' organizations, women's groups, and non-governmental organizations are important sources of innovation and action at the local level and have a strong interest and proven ability to promote sustainable livelihoods. Governments, in cooperation with appropriate international and non-governmental organizations should support a community-driven approach to sustainability..." (UN Conference on Environment and Development, Agenda 21, 1992)

4. "Existing inequalities and barriers to women in the workforce should be eliminated and women's participation in all policy-making and implementation as well as their access to productive resources, and ownership of land and their right to inherit property should be promoted and strengthened." (Beijing Platform for Action, UN Fourth World Conference on Women 1995)

Keeping governments accountable at the NGO Forum (1995)

The common denominator in these UN documents is the message that social equity, gender justice, and human rights are the real purpose of economic growth. The UN meetings that followed since these social development conferences of the 1990s have repeated and re-committed to the same principles. The question remains: why are we still talking about a stand-alone goal for gender equality and the need to mainstream gender into economic planning? Economists must be qualified to put gender equality into the long string of sound bytes that make up UN recommendations. If they do not, they may not be the best managers of women taxpayers' dollars.

Exploiting Our Children

Bees have a language. Sea otters are great inventors of tools. Gorillas have lifelong family ties and may even fall in love. What makes human beings different from other animals?

There is only one outstanding characteristic that sets humans apart from other animals, although we should hardly be proud to admit it. As far as I know, we are the only species to make slaves of our own offspring.

According to the ILO (https://www.ilo.org/global/topics/child-labour/lang--en/index.htm), 168 million of the world's children work. They make soccer balls and carpets for export. Children are also domestic workers, brick-makers, peddlers, and garbage pickers. Although most child laborers live in developing countries and work in agriculture, there are also many children employed in industrialized countries.

These figures do not reveal the numbers of children who are bonded servants, sexually exploited, physically disabled due to accidents, or exposed to hazardous chemicals. Yet, such conditions are known to prevail in the businesses that hire children. Child soldiers are among

Bangladeshi Child working in the fields

the most abused workers. Furthermore, the exploitation of the girl-child is hidden because no one counts daily household tasks as unpaid labor. The Beijing Platform for Action policy document adopted in 1995 at the UN Fourth World Conference on Women declared the plight of the girl-child as one of the Twelve Critical Areas of Concern.

It's not that human nature is evil. Employers' motives range from benevolence to pure profit. Particularly if they are relatives, and those who hire children may see their gesture as a rescue operation to save the young from unscrupulous exploiters. Others are less charitable. Like lords in feudal domains, the employers decide the rules. Political and economic structures in place provide no guaranteed safeguards for children. The owners' personal inclinations determine whether there are fair wages or safe work conditions, rather than follow child labor laws.

Another unknown is why parents send children to work in the first place. Many critics would say that parents are driven by profit. Of course, there are some who cold-heartedly sell their children like unwanted animals. On the other hand, most parents are themselves victims of circumstances: homeless, impoverished and unemployed. Refugees may seek security for daughters and marry them off in return for payment to local nationals. There is very little information about how children are pushed out of their nests into the wild to fend for themselves. It is known that sometimes, middlemen dupe rural families with promises of finding jobs for their daughters. Instead, these middle men sell the girls into prostitution. In other cases, the change from subsistence to cash economies puts pressure on families to earn wages. Everyone has to pitch in, and older children may work to help support everyone else. In cities, work can be the lesser of two evils; youth who are employed can avoid a life of crime.

There are many questions. Did any of these families really have options? Why are there so many unwanted children in the first place? If women had control over their fertility, wouldn't they be able to reduce the supply of poor children flowing into the labor market?

One thing is certain. Modern human beings may not be born bad, but they need strong political and legal constraints to remind them of their moral responsibilities. There are standards and conventions that upload these constraints: the ILO conventions, the UNICEF Convention on the Rights of the Child, the Convention on the Elimination of All Forms of Discrimination against Women (CEDAW), and other international agreements. Granted, a child is not likely to take an employer to court to defend their rights. Labor laws are not easy to enforce because many child laborers work in homes and the informal sector. Yet, these conventions are essential to raise society's standards for decent human behavior.

The voyage from public awareness to the enforcement of child labor laws may be wild and woolly, but it is well worth the political struggle. If child labor is banished, we would take a progressive step forward in human evolution that may be as significant as the domestication of animals. We will have tamed our own exploitative nature and the base human instinct of self-interest.

What Do Rural Women Really Want?

Millions of families spend a lifetime trying to get it. Many people feud bitterly when they do. For many older people, they would rather die than let an outsider buy it. No, we're not talking about family jewels here but something more important: land. Fertile or meager, rocky or rich—just land.

For most of the world's small farmers, land is like a healthy savings account. It assures social and economic security, provides access to get credit, and can be sold in hard times as a last resort. In many rural cultures, land ownership is also a matter of respect and dignity. It can affirm a family's sense of belonging in the community and bind two generations together in a time-honored transaction. If you give your land to the eldest son, he can care for you in your old age. UN Women reports that when women own land, they are less likely to experience violence at home and have more voice in how to spend family income (Realizing Women's Rights to Land, UN Women, 2013).

So, what happens to landless women? The noted feminist economist Bina Agawal reports that there are many cases in India and Bangladesh where widows and divorcees end up working as agricultural

• Rural women in Nepalese market

laborers on the farms of their well-off brothers or brothers-in-law. Even the women who run their husband's farms while their husbands work elsewhere have few rights, if any. They are unable to improve production, get credit, or adopt new technologies—all because they do not control the land they cultivate.

In Africa, women produce 70 percent of the continent's foodstuffs. Yet, women own less than two percent of the world's land. In countries like Brazil and Kenya, landholdings for women are smaller in size and value than those of men. Ironically, the so-called feminization of poverty has become more lopsided as women's responsibility for food production is increasing.

That's only part of the bad news. When prices for water supplies go up, or structural adjustment leads to cuts in health services, poor rural women suffer the most. As their scarce resources are already spread thin, the whole family's living standard are also lowered. Spending on food, health, and basic needs is more likely to come from women's earnings. Unfortunately, men in similar situations are more likely to spend extra money on their personal needs, such as tobacco and liquor.

Land remains key to women's success. When women control land, they reap social and economic benefits. Indian women in the Bodhgaya region reported that there were more family crises involving drunkenness and wife-beating in communities where only men had the titles during land reform. Where women received titles, the relationship between men and women improved. As the women put it, "We had tongues, but could not speak. We had feet, but could not walk. Now that we have land, we have the strength to speak and walk."

Delegates from 181 countries at the 1995 UN Fourth World Conference on Women in Beijing pledged to work toward giving rural women the power to speak and walk. The Beijing Platform for Action endorses the idea that all women have the equal right to inheritance an important symbolic step. However, that is only a start. Land is the first bank account that rural women need.

Shoes and Economic Miracles

My first experience in foreign aid was in the 1950s when I helped my parents send shoes to Korean orphans. The orphanage director wrote that the Korean War had wiped out the shoemaking business. If charitable Americans could donate used shoes, children could survive the winter. Within a year, aromatic mountains of faded sneakers, crumbled slip-ons, and boots filled the attic. We sent them all, knowing that some would be sold to buy food.

Nearly 25 years later, South Korea was one of the world's major exporters of shoes. You could go through piles of shoes on sale in the East Gate Market to find the real bargains. With per capita incomes that had increased more than 150 percent, most Koreans could also buy the goods they made.

Economists have tried to draw lessons from the Korean pattern of development. They are particularly intrigued by the close interaction between improvements in human development and economic growth. South Korea's near-100 percent literacy rate in the 1990s compared favorably with highly industrialized nations. By 1993, Korea's poorest 20 percent had about one third the average per capita

Jeju island women are the backbone of the economy

income compared with the poor in the United States, where they had less than one fourth the average income per capita.

Most economists acknowledge that Korea's success was not due to a trickle-down effect from economic growth to social welfare. South Korea's economy became a prime example of how a resource-poor country can compete in international markets with export-oriented strategies, starting with social, not economic, development. On the eve of its economic take off, South Korea had already reduced its population growth rate. It also had a large pool of skilled labor that included women and girls and had a critical mass of expertise in science and technology.

However, try as they may, many struggling countries in sub-Saharan Africa and Latin America cannot replicate the Korean economic experience. Maybe they have focused too hard on numbers and not enough on the process. Political will may be more important than we ever imagined.

In the South Korean situation, political will at all levels was a major determinant of its economic direction. Korean economists promoted and won support for economic growth policies based on equitable investments in education for the rural poor, including girls. They also successfully argued for public sector spending to upgrade rural life, so a woman's time and work would be reduced. Investments were made in rural health services and family planning. The Korean National Economic Planning Board carefully monitored rural-urban income distribution, and the transfer of private wealth into public coffers was required.

At the international level, global financial institutions and the United States cooperated to create an international financial and trade structure that favored South Korea's entry into the global economy of labor-intensive, export-oriented industries. These areas favored the employment of girls in the electronics and garment industries.

Korean national policy probably would have failed without the political will for equity from the bottom-up. Democracy and labor movements of the 1970s and 1980s among students, factory workers, women, and farmers made economic justice a development issue. Their gains were won at high political costs, and, at times, with their lives. Chun Tae-Il was only 22 years old when he burned himself to death in protest of the harsh working conditions of textile workers in the sweatshops of Youngdeungpo district. Factory girls went on strike repeatedly for fairer wages and better work and living conditions in free trade zones. They were strongly supported by women human rights leaders and the Christian Industrial Mission. Rural women asserted their economic and political leadership against the tide of authoritarian rule.

These democratic rumblings and disturbances were the key ingredients in creating a stronger, more peaceful transition to an open economy governed by democratic principles. We need to take stock of this turbulent political chapter in Korea's economic history. We should treasure the social and political sacrifices, commemorate the legacies of the democratic and labor movements, and remind political leaders that all of the above ultimately laid a strong foundation for sustainable economic growth.

Lessons from a Swiss Village

I once went to an anthropology conference on European peasants in a Swiss village on the remote slopes of a beautiful mountain. In the heart of industrialized Europe, a hearty, traditional, peasant way of life had survived—or so we thought. The small Swiss house where I stayed was run by an elderly woman whose cheek colors matched the reddest strawberries I had ever seen, piled high on the breakfast table. Strawberries were among the few cash crops that made it out to the cities. The rest of the fruits and vegetables were destined for old-fashion home cooking. Madame served us vegetables that she grew in her backyard. She also produced cheese and fruit products that were often used for friendly barter. Her vineyards were outstanding examples of artisanal care.

I thought this was idyllic living until I noticed something strange a few days later. I rarely met a young person. The statistics were right. Like poor villages throughout western Europe, the migration of rural youth in Switzerland to cities had resulted in a serious drain of labor from rural areas. Higher education and jobs expanded opportunities for youth in cities, but they also meant that newer generations were abandoning villages. What escaped the eyes of policymakers is that these children also left their parents behind.

The UN needs to pay attention to the plight of rural women, particularly older rural women because their numbers are increasing. In agricultural communities where retirement exists only if children take over responsibilities, older women must now work longer hours just to survive. Globally, the situation is worse because only 10 to 20 percent of all landholders are women.[1] When disasters strike, such as prolonged droughts, older women find it harder to access credit and other resources to rebuild their farmlands. This is a loss for the whole of society. The FAO estimates that if women had the same access to productive resources as men, they could increase yields on their farms by 20 to 30 percent, contributing to end to world hunger.[2]

Even in wealthy, developed countries, women farmers live in the south of the north. Like many of their counterparts in developing countries, these women have lower rates of literacy, poorer health, and less access to modern communications than the average citizen. We would learn a lot if the older women of this Swiss village were invited to sit among us at the United Nations and judge progress from their point of view.

---

1 FAO, The State of food and Agriculture: Women in Agriculture, closing the Gender Gap for Development, Rome 2011 and http://www.fao.org/3/i2050e/i2082e00.pdf

2 Ibid

Packing the UN for Davos

As heads of state pack their bags for the annual World Economic Forum in Davos, Switzerland, there are a few essential documents they should pack in their briefcases. They should pack UN treaties that discuss the rights to economic development, social equities, and human rights. It may not be easy to get the papers together; the documents are likely in the hands of bureaucrats or have already been marked for the archives. However, these papers are excellent references for the Davos discussions on the future of the world economy.

While UN treaties are known to deal with jurisprudence and international law, they have much richer political meaning. The treaty ratification process requires states to determine how a global ethical standard, such as human rights, applies to specific issues around hiring practices and business management. That connection is unlikely to materialize unless world leaders outside of the UN circle are aware that these documents exist.

Two treaties with particular relevance to the majority of the world's poor, especially women and children, are the following:

- **Convention on the Elimination of All Forms of Discrimination against Women (CEDAW):** As of 2018, the Convention was ratified by 188 countries (although not by the US) and went into force in 1981. It is often described as an international bill of rights for women. Article 11 of CEDAW ensures that state parties take all appropriate measures to eliminate discrimination against women in the field of employment. It also guarantees them their rights to work, free choice of profession, promotion, job security, remuneration in respect of work of equal value" Other provisions include the right to social security, health and safety in the workplace. More articles provide broad social and political rights, such as the right to education, health, and political participation.
- **Convention on the Rights of the Child (CRC).** The CRC is outstanding in international law as the most broadly ratified treaty ever. Currently only two member states have not ratified the CRC: The United States and Somalia. The 191 countries that stand behind the CRC have affirmed the principle of non-discrimination on the basis of race, color, gender, language, religion, opinion, origin, disability, birth or any other characteristic. The CRC also provides a framework to defend children's rights as universal, indivisible, and interdependent–all of which are essential elements to rally national support for children's welfare and end child labor.

Presidents and prime ministers may have left their homes in haste on their way to Davos, but that should not get in the way of making sure that their preparations are adequate. The treaties should be considered quasi-personal travel items. After all, their signatures and those of their eminent predecessors adorn them. Heads of state must accept personal responsibility for these treaties in order to get CEOs in the private sector to take an interest.

A Beginner's Poverty Index

I recently learned that healthcare workers in Los Angeles had carried out the biggest unionization drive since 1937, gathering together 74,000 home care workers. Ironically, one of their demands was their own access to health insurance. It was sobering to learn that the women home care workers, who feed, bathe, and clean the elderly and disabled, weren't covered by health insurance themselves. They did not have paid vacations, or any other benefits normally allotted to full-time workers in the healthcare system.

Something churns inside when you realize that what you do for a living yields such low wages and social benefits that you can't afford the goods or services you produce. You don't need complex mathematical equations or quantitative indicators to figure out what constitutes fairness or economic deprivation.

There might be a lesson here for experts who try to measure poverty. They still struggle around identifying markers for economic justice or the right to development, so I suggest we use common sense when science fails. I have my own rapid assessment indicators of social and economic development related to women's welfare.

• Poor homes in Kashmir, India

One indicator is what I call the "milk indicator." Dairy cooperatives in India have done wonders to raise family incomes. Groups of women tend to the cows, carry heavy loads of feed, and keep the cows healthy. Children play around the animals and watch them produce a plentiful day's worth of milk. However, poor women must sell the milk to buy food and other necessities, so many of them must deny their children the very milk they produce. To me, that is an indicator of social deprivation.

Another indicator is what I call the "third world egg indicator." In many poor countries, well-meaning healthcare workers offer nutritional advice to mothers and recommend to feed the children eggs. In reality, eggs and chickens are often a luxury. They can be so valuable that the poorest farmers sell them to buy grain. I think that a country's agricultural development policies are failing if farmers cannot afford to eat the foods they produce.

A third indicator is a technology indicator. Household surveyors should ask female electronic workers if they can afford to have televisions. In many developing countries, such luxury items are strictly for the wealthy. In fact, they can be so expensive that entire villages may share just one television. Young women who work in electronic industries in developing countries often live in the pre-industrial world of crowded housing and squalor. They help assemble complex electronic equipment that connect a global communications system, yet they themselves cannot afford to access that world themselves.

Let us create a world where those who contribute to a country's prosperity do not face the indignity of economic deprivation daily. Let us also use real people's experiences in UN indicators to measure progress.

The Myth of the Hunter

Man as the fearless hunter is a popular, but unfounded myth about prehistoric society. In this mistaken view, early men braved the wilds to provide most of the family's food. They supposedly hunted hairy mammoths and brought home wild pig bacon. Men made and shaped culture. They were the great ones in control.

Of course, a variation of this myth portrays men as the sole inventors of fire, tools, and language. In this myth, the women's primary role was to support the men's primary food-providing activities, remain silent partners, and aspire to be ideal mothers. They were presumed to be the weaker sex who stayed close to the home fires in order to protect, cook, and care for the hunters.

Many fundamentalist religious groups embrace this skewed interpretation of human history. There is no doubt this allows them to declare that there is little contradiction between scientific theories of evolution and religious writings. In the eyes of fundamentalists, God in all His wisdom instilled a social lesson in the biological differences and traditional power relationships between the sexes. Feminists who do not accept biological determination are said to go against the dictates of natural history and divine will.

In the opposite camp, anthropologists who have argued that early human society was more egalitarian. They view the main food providers as women, not men. Recent archeological findings at Neolithic sites confirm that most early Homo sapiens did not depend on large animals for food. The scorched beast was only an occasional treat. The real staple foods were roots, nuts, fruits, small game, and other less glamorous comestibles. Far from huddling by the fire, women probably had to roam the grasslands and forests to hunt for animals with nets and gather foodstuffs. All of this activity required as much physical endurance as chasing big game. The most recent anthropological findings also suggest that women very likely domesticated plants and invented tools for food processing and storage.

Family planning was part of women's lives too. Anthropologists report that contemporary hunting and gathering groups such as the !Kung Bushmen of the Kalihari Desert used traditional techniques to reduce family size through prolonged breastfeeding, abortion, herbal contraceptives, and abstinence. !Kung women knew that they could not wander over large areas of land if they had to carry small children. To adapt to the need for mobility, they limited the numbers of children to around five. There were wide intervals between births with an average spacing of three to four year per child.

In brief, almost everything we know about the social and economic life of hunters and gatherers refutes the idea that motherhood was women's primary role in the beginning. It is also unlikely that she was a passive participant in a man's world. The question is why the old myth of man, the hunter, persists despite published scientific evidence for several decades. The only possible explanation is sheer stubbornness. Some people find it convenient to disregard scientific evidence because they use the past to justify the present. There is one person in anthropological circles who is absolutely delighted about this: man, the hunter.

Economic Man Dressed in Women's Clothes

No one laughs when the economic man comes on stage. He plays his part seriously and well. He's an old timer in the drama of development conferences. Few delegations bother questioning why he was chosen to play the lead role. His portrayal of human character is familiar and appears to be at the liking of most people in the audience.

The role requires him to bring to life the average underdog of development: the peasants, the unemployed, and the landless. These characters are all male of course. He plays other parts equally well. The economic man can be heroic as he swiftly and inexorably moves to reach every national target on time in response to the proper market incentives. The problem is that this rational, predictable character doesn't resemble anyone we know.

Above all, the basic market-driven economic man is a two-dimensional petty entrepreneur and insatiable consumer. Common sense suggests that something is missing. Perhaps it's his emphasis on placing value children's education instead of one's own career or the inclination to share with a neighbor. The economic man never strays far from center stage of profit-seeking and personal gain. He wins the national theater awards every year.

The illusion that everyone has a place in classic economic theories has some merit. We now acknowledge that women are often the main breadwinners and heads of household and that sustainable development policies are also a women's issue. Similarly, our image of children has evolved as we begin to see them as child laborers or as the exploited work force behind the textile and electronics industries. These advances in our view of the typical active participant in development can only go so far. Our understanding remains skewed by the predominant assumption that women and children are only minor variations of the same old economic man.

The absurdity of this fiction comes clear in a review of projects designed to improve women's condition. Activist women's groups have argued for some time that many women are powerless to respond to market incentives in the same way as men can. For example, in order to attract more young mothers to health centers, health fees may be lowered. Mothers may know that they should go to the health center for prenatal examinations, but they may not be allowed to travel alone in public. In societies where women are not considered social adults, they must ask permission to leave the house. Health decisions are made for them, often against their own interests.

To be like the economic man, women must also have the power to make decisions regarding their own incomes. The Beijing Platform for Action calls for governments to recognize that women's decision-making power must start in the home. Married women may be active members of the work force, but if they are acting on a husband's or a father's order, they are not fully integrated participants in the economy. They run head-on into social costs that hurt a lot—literally—as husbands living in traditional, patriarchal societies may resort to violence if wives do not hand over their earnings.

Even if family members do not control women's economic behavior, poor women may not have access to mass media and information networks that provide necessary economic know-hows, like the best market prices. Most women traders do not have critical information required to react to new economic opportunities. They even may be illiterate and unable to cope with banking procedures to access credit even when available. Let us also state the obvious. They have to understand credit schemes in order to take advantage of them.

The differences in economic behavior go deeper. There is increasing evidence that when they have the voice to speak up in household economic decisions, women are more likely to show more altruistic economic behavior than men. They may go without medicine for the sake of their children or elderly parents. Studies by the World Bank (https://www.worldbank.org/en/topic/gender) show that given the freedom to choose, women are more likely to spend money on goods and services that raise the family's living standard. Men's expenditures are much more likely to be on social life and luxury goods.

We would be gravely misled to focus entirely on market-oriented strategies without taking a second look at the social and cultural parameters of human behavior. Basic assumptions behind economic policies, particularly those that affect women, should come under gender scrutiny. The Beijing Platform for Action calls for women's economic empowerment as a means to lift society in its entirety out of poverty. It can't work to just let economic man dress in women's clothes.

Let Them Eat Chocolate

General MacArthur's statue in the Whitney Museum stood nearly eight feet tall, his knuckles resting confidently on his hips. His eyes looked sharp, as if he were inspecting you rather than you gazing at him. The larger-than-life statue was a reminder that this man had once wielded uncommon power. With a wave of his hand, he decided the fate of thousands of American soldiers and millions of Koreans during the Korean War.

Memories of American soldiers who served under him hung on the walls, hundreds of small, rectangular blocks bearing the stripes of uniform badges. The dark brown sculpture material added to a mood of solemn silence. Too many soldiers died in what's called the "forgotten war." This artistic memorial to the Korean War was long overdue.

When I looked closer at the general's elbow, there was a sweet, yet pungent, smell. It was coming from his cuff, his jacket, and the walls. It was the brown stuff of children's dreams and Christmas cheer, none other than the wonderful smell of dark chocolate. For many Korean children who were starving during the war, it was also the scent of America.

• Kang Ik-Joong, multi-media installation artist (2017)

The brilliant artist, Kang Ik-Joong, justified his reason for choosing chocolate as the material for his monument. As he explains it, some of his clearest childhood memories were of good-willed American soldiers throwing chocolate bars to children. The soldiers shared some of the most exotic goods imaginable. The children's favorite was gum because its flavor lasted forever. Candy went down quicker. Many children hoarded gum and candy wrappers for weeks, smelling them over and over again to relive that satisfying moment.

It is ironic that candy and gum should be the enduring memories of starvation. However, when one is very hungry, the first taste of anything is wonderful and unforgettable. Taste is a conduit to childhood memories. Sadly, for today's children in war-torn countries, like Afghanistan, Somalia and Rwanda, these memories may best be forgotten.

According to UNICEF annual report in 2016, there were 25 million children displaced due to conflict. Two years later, that number increased to an estimated 30 million children. In the past decade, nearly two million children have been killed in wars, many of whom died of diseases related to malnutrition and a lack of safe water and sanitation. Their own armies have sold international relief goods for arms while children have waited for food aid that never arrived due to embargoes.

At the annual UN High-level Political Forum, heads of state and ministers report on how their countries progress toward achieving sustainable development goals. While food security, nutrition, and health are central to measuring whether or not these are successful, few governments report on how wars are undermining progress. Unless we invest more in forging peace, refugees will feel that the meetings produce more sweet talk than action.

Follow the Money

In the midst of the Watergate scandal, the anonymous source Deep Throat urged Bob Woodward and Carl Bernstein of *The Washington Post*, to forget all the other distractions and "follow the money." They took the advice, and it ultimately led them to unravel the political intrigue behind Watergate.

What was true for the young media watchdogs is equally relevant to other political situations. Resolutions and campaign promises aside, the real story of the politics of development is where the money is coming from, where it is going, and what it is supposed to achieve. For poor, rural women and girls, the burden of missteps falls on them the hardest. Ask any girls in a mountainous Nepalese village if she has seen UN funds, and she is likely to respond with puzzled looks.

At the annual UN High-level Political Forum, the hope that the private sector would kick in additional resources to make up for shrinking government spending hasn't been realized yet. The trends in the UN budget crisis are not encouraging. Many women were shocked to learn that the promise of additional resources at the Fourth World Conference on Women was followed only six months

Nepalese girls carry heavy burdens

later by drastic cuts in the UN's budget for women's programs.

The question remains: does any money reach those who need it? If not, why not?

Here are some answers. At the level of international assistance, high-level corruption may result in goods being siphoned off to private warehouses and cash being spirited away to Swiss bank accounts. However, fraud and mismanagement ultimately bite the hands that feed them. Isolationists and conservatives can cite them as reasons for not giving taxpayers' money to the UN. Similarly, the abuse of public funds supports arguments for a turn to privatization. However, the private sector seldom shows an inclination to help the poorest of the poor. As a result, the flow of money slows to a trickle, and the oil fields of international funding dry up.

The little public money available is often channeled indiscriminately at the national level. Grants are given to small town and village development projects for political reasons and without regard to who is really controlling the funds. In community and household-based data, gross averages hide income disparities within communities. The money flows to the well-organized or well-connected, not necessarily where it is needed the most. Women's groups are no exception. In more than a few countries, elite women also monopolize access to critical resources.

Does the money have a positive effect? It often depends on the structure of how funds are allocated. A classic example concerns how national health programs were designed to reduce maternal mortality. A ministry of health decides to make maternal mortality a high priority. However, rather than fund programs that could have a positive impact on poor, rural women and girls, local politics sways the health department to build expensive, high-tech health centers in the capital. If there are funds left over, a new machine is purchased. In this scenario, everyone is happy. The politicians get their pictures in the paper at the ribbon-cutting. A few well-to-do patients get access to modern medicine. However, the health prospects of most mothers aren't changed at all. There is simply no money left over to provide supplies to provincial hospitals or to establish community emergency transport for villagers.

Financing for development is a feminist issue. The current trends show that gender-blind economic policies continue to undervalue women's unpaid work. One solution would be to demand that governments make their accounts public for all to scrutinize. If we are to be serious at the UN, we need to address the issue of money from the very beginning. In the midst of all the distractions and rhetoric of sustainable development debates, there must be straight talk about cash and how we can be more accountable for its uses.

Education—an Enduring Gift

When I was a child, my aunt used to say, "Your education is the only wealth you will have for life. Wars can destroy your home, and someone might steal your land, but no one can take away what you have learned."

She often used a diplomatic tone to disguise a hard scolding, so I thought she was only urging me to get better grades. Her own diplomas were framed and hung prominently over the fireplace of the home library. It was well known among her friends that she loved studying. When my aunt died at the age of 94, she and her husband donated the bulk of their wealthy estate to the University of Michigan as a reminder to others that there are some things money can—and should—buy. She believed that girl's rights to education was an inalienable human right. It is also a girl's best chance for a life free from poverty.

When I told a Polish friend about my aunt's advice, we discovered that her grandmother and my aunt were remarkably like-minded. Her grandmother, also a doctor, had fled Lithuania to escape communist repression. Courageously traveling mostly by foot, it took her

• SDG Goal 4. Education (2021)

months to reach Poland because armies detained her to help the wounded. We exchanged stories about how refugees leave home in confusion and panic. My friend said, "Do you know the only thing my grandmother took with her when she left? It was her school diploma."

Asians are known for their traditional veneration of education. In Korean and Chinese traditions, scholars had a higher status than generals or businessmen. However, reverence for education is more prevalent in other cultures than we think. Mexicans, Russians, and many others drive their children to succeed in their studies and teach them to respect their teachers. Although such values are virtuous, a double standard that bars girls from the school yard is still widespread. In many villages, I have seen girls carrying infants, fetching water, and doing household chores in order for their brothers to attend school. The problem is not just narrow-minded parents. Girls who venture out on the road to attend school may be attacked. In highly traditional cultures, educating girls makes them much harder to marry off because dowries rise with years of schooling.

Better news comes from the United States, where the imbalance between girls and boys at the primary school level has been equalized for many years. This is largely because women battled for girls' rights to education years ago.

Investing in education is simply smart planning because it builds long-term social and economic reserves that can be drawn upon when times are hard. This is not to imply that education is useful only as a social life insurance policy. As development planners are fond of pointing out, there are sound arguments that education—including girls' education—helps to build strong economies as well. For women and the poor, the security of education has no parallel. Human tragedies strike when least expected, and they often hit women and girls the hardest. For millions of women refugees, their education may be the only jewel they can safely carry to freedom.

In a Chinese Kitchen, It's Still a Man's World

During a follow-up meeting to a Beijing women's conference in China, I joined a group excursion to the Jinsong Vocational School, which was renowned for producing China's top fashion designers and master chefs. We looked forward to learning about the programs that promoted girls' education. We wondered if schools could alter the age-old gender stereotypes about women's work. In theory, schools should be the first places for re-socializing the next generation with the ideals of gender equality. In practice, matters can take a different turn. The Jinsong School was a prime example of that.

At first glance, the School was impressive with its modern architecture and first-rate facilities. The classroom seats overlooked an elaborate model kitchen. There were heavy knives that could lop off a chicken's neck—or a careless finger—with a single swing. Stainless steel cooking utensils lay in order like surgical instruments next to drum-sized woks. We could clearly see the tops of counters and stoves from an ingenious V-shaped mirror on the wall that captured everything below from a bird's-eye view. It was a well-planned stage to showcase a master's skills.

The chef entered the room like a head physician leading his interns. Dressed in white coats and trim cooking hats, the students stood proudly as China's culinary crème de la crème. Their teacher's tall hat elevated his stature to a wondrous and authoritative height. We stared as they stood before us for a brief inspection. There was something odd about this class of students: They were all boys. The teacher also was of prime male stock. Where were the girls?

There was much whispering in the crowd but not much protest. In the interest of letting the chef demonstrate how to cook Szechuan chili chicken with peanuts, we let this touchy issue pass. We were promised a cooking lesson followed by a tasting feast, and this soothed us into a cooperative mood. There would be plenty of time to talk about gender equality later.

The master chef awed us with his skill. Three chickens had been de-boned and cubed to mathematical precision. He deftly spilled the heaps of meat into the large wok for deep-frying. With the help of his students, he picked up the heavy pan and drained off the oil. He added chopped ginger, garlic, onions, and Chinese herbs. Cornstarch and water were soon followed by peanuts. Much to our surprise, he threw in a dash of ketchup. (He later confided that this was a nouvelle cuisine touch he added just for foreigners.) We were all writing down the recipe furiously, noting important details like the correct temperature for frying. Suddenly, flames leaped up from the sides of the pan. To the chef's delight, we gasped with amazement. He smiled and calmly tipped the pan to reduce the flames. It was a routine gesture in a master chef's performance.

Afterwards came the question-and-answer session. A woman asked, "Do you also teach cooking to girls?"

"No," he answered. "Cooking takes a lot of muscle and stamina, and it is much more suitable for boys." We could hardly believe our ears. The Jinsong School admissions tests screened out boys who didn't look strong enough to be cooks. On the other hand, the most attractive girls were admitted to the School as fashion designers.

There were no female cooking students.

"What do you do at home?" asked another woman. "Do you cook, or does your wife have to do it all?" The mood was changing into a feminist inquisition. The chef answered that since he cooks all day at school, he hardly feels like doing it when he gets home. He lets his wife take over that job.

The questions continued. Someone asked if the administrators would allow a girl to pursue a cooking diploma if she wanted to learn to cook. The school director explained that each student can freely choose his or her program; however, girls don't take up cooking because it was considered heavy work and too hard. The School also thought that it was unlikely that women chefs could get a job after graduation. In China, hotel and restaurant kitchens were part of a man's world.

Maybe we should have been more understanding. After all, this prejudice against women chefs is not unique to China. Most famous chefs are men, even in France. Men and women may do the same job, but male chefs get high wages and praise. Women get the unpaid drudgery of daily meals. We suggested that a cultural revolution in China to promote equal work opportunities for women has to start somewhere and that a famous institution like Jinsong is a perfect place to kick it off. The school's teachers and administrators acknowledged this sage advice with a polite smile.

As we left, I spied a group of women cooks behind the school canteen peeling vegetables. I wondered whether any of them had attended the lecture on Szechuan chili chicken with peanuts. If not, they were being deprived of a wonderful experience. Pity that the rules of tradition held fast even in a modern vocational school. Here, as elsewhere, boys are groomed to become famous chefs, while women are the dutiful assistants on the sidelines.

Chapter 7

Collective Voices

"Empowering women as political and social actors can change policy choices."

_ The World Bank

Introduction

If Eleanor Roosevelt's ghost could speak at the UN today, she probably would have eloquent but stern words for world leaders. A pioneer in the struggle for women's rights, she wouldn't have missed a chance to remind them that the UN would not be an outstanding institution without women's leadership. However, many governments seem to have forgotten her story of the UN. While women's leadership is prominent in social sectors, the trade and finance negotiations at the UN remain dominated by men.

Still, progress has been made. When the UN Charter was signed in 1945, only 47 countries guaranteed women the right to vote. There was no national legislation banning female genital mutilation. Sexism was an unknown diplomatic term, and women had never written an international treaty. Change was inevitable as women leaders took an active interest in international politics. Furthermore, that momentum had been building within the women's movements long before the UN was founded.

In 1919, the National Women's Trade Union League convened the first International Congress of Working Women in Washington,

• Beijing + 20 during CSW in New York (2015)

D.C. in cooperation with its European counterpart. They worked to adopt labor measures, such as the *Convention on Maternity Protection* and laws concerning night work and minimum wage for women. At a meeting of the League of Nations, a woman on the Danish delegation succeeded in drawing the organization's attention to the plight of women and children deported from Turkey. By 1937, the concern for women's legal rights and claims to nationality were strong enough for the League of Nations Assembly to establish a Committee of Experts on the Legal Status of Women.

During the negotiations on the UN Charter, feisty women delegates from Brazil, the Dominican Republic, and Mexico insisted that the phrase "to ensure respect for human rights and fundamental freedoms without discrimination against race, sex, condition or creed" be included in the UN Charter and enshrined in the Universal Declaration of Human Rights.

Soon afterwards, Eleanor Roosevelt, who was an American delegate to the first General Assembly, met with a handful of government representatives and signed the proclamation, *Open Letter to the Women of the World*. This document encouraged women to take more active roles in international affairs and the peace movement. Many delegates also argued that the UN needed to establish an independent body for women's affairs.

Events moved quickly. In May 1946, a sub-commission of the Economic and Social Council (ECOSOC) approved a set of principles, policies, and a thirteen-point program for a separate commission on women. Later that year, with the strong support of the United States, ECOSOC established the most important UN body responsible for overseeing policies concerning women: the Commission on the Status of Women (CSW).

For more than half a century, the world's women have claimed a political space on UN territory. Like creative landscape architects, the women's movement has sketched ambitious plans. In 2020, the UN celebrated the 25th anniversary of the UN Fourth World Conference

• CSW colleagues: Krishanti Dharmaraj, Charlotte Bunch, Bani Dugal and Susan O'Malley at CSW (2019)

on Women—the largest conference ever held in the history of the UN. Then, during the Beijing + 25 celebrations we created the Feminist and Women's Movement Action Plan to support the UN work for generation equality. Women have done their part. But have governments delivered?

NGO Forum on Women 1995

Let's not be modest. With nearly 50 thousand NGO and government participants, the Fourth World Conference on Women qualified for the *Guinness Book of Records* as the largest number of women activists working together at any one place ever. If we had all jumped at once on Huairou ground, we might have knocked the earth out of its orbit.

The NGO Forum on Women began days before the official conference. For ten days, participants chose from 4,000 workshops and panels to attend. They joined in the daily plenaries that highlighted speeches from feminist activists and leaders. Plenary speakers rallied the crowds around global themes, such as political participation, religious freedom, economic justice, and violence against women. Tents for women to meet each other according to the world's regions were the centers of networking and lobbying preparations.

Youths, the disabled, lesbians, and indigenous peoples had their own tents. Electronic technology was used effectively to link the Forum to the UN conference and to a global townhouse. There were more than 60,000 emails sent and received and around 100,000 visits to the NGO Forum website. (Imagine what that number would be if the UN conference happened today).

There was no doubt about it. In both virtual and real spaces, this was a global conference like no other. The international women's movement in Beijing appeared stronger, more diverse, and more committed to influencing the UN than ever before. The interaction between non-governmental organizations (NGOs) and governments had passed many milestones since the first UN women's conference in Mexico in 1975. From Copenhagen (1980) to Nairobi (1985), we saw the evolution of the NGO Forum from a rebel camp on the outskirts of the UN grounds to a legitimate partner inside the UN tent.

Global paradigms and international consciousness had also evolved. In the past two decades leading up to the NGO Forum, the women's movement had branched out to take an active interest in major UN social development summits on population, poverty, racism, and the environment. International networks, working groups, and national women's organizations had lobbied to bring a women's agenda to the attention of world leaders. The political momentum of these meetings finally converged in Beijing. By then, the discourse had shifted from viewing women as victims to an assertion of women's rights as fellow citizens.

The Huairou NGO Forum was a full partner with the official meeting more than any other UN conference. The success of the Fourth World Conference on Women depended on the strong interaction and mutual commitments between NGOs and governments. The NGO and government interaction shaped the political dynamics that led to a global consensus document known as the Beijing Platform for Action (BPfA).

One critical point: the women's conferences were not just events. They were highlights of a long political process which shifted its leadership from women of the North to women representing a global, regional-based movement. Nor was the BPfA just another UN document; what distinguished this lengthy paper from previous plans of

• The NGO Forum organizing team in New York (1993)

action was the invisible transformation of the NGO-government political process that led to the compromises represented within the BPfA. The real Post-Beijing legacy was a structural change in the relationship of a social movement to the intergovernmental system.

The size, scope, and goals of the NGO Forum on Women presented new organizing challenges that required innovations in the broader organizational structure. To meet this challenge, Supatra Masdit and Irene Santiago, the Forum's convener and executive director respectively, were determined to organize regional facilitating committees and coordinate these committees through a full-time secretariat in New York.

A critical factor leading to the success of the NGO Forum was the collaboration between the facilitating committee and a new NGO Forum Secretariat. While a handful of women had organized previous women's conferences representing international NGOs and basing the meetings in the United States, this NGO Forum had roots throughout the world and was culturally diverse. Regional focal points, backed by representatives from the Conference of Non-Governmental Organizations (COnGO), and the NGO Committees on the Status of Women worked with the New York Secretariat. With a Planning Committee of 200 organizations, these groups raised funds, organized the regional NGO Forums, helped coordinate the women's caucuses, and provided technical support to the regions. A newsletter kept everyone informed and shared helpful guidelines on how to draft amendments to the official UN documents.

In New York, I joined a small team that constituted the Secretariat along with a dedicated group of volunteers and interns. My job was to liaise with the UN and help coordinate regional NGOs. Using the best of high-tech equipment and communications available at the time, our group was able to manage the complexities of a global conference. Most of us had left our own jobs to join the team. At the beginning, we did not realize that we had entered an endless maze of new challenges.

It all started smoothly. The 14-member NGO facilitating committee had returned from their first visit to China with a written agreement that guaranteed freedom of speech on NGO Forum grounds. With the site issue settled, we turned to the problem of raising our own funds, since the UN did not sponsor or fund the NGO Forum. There was reason to be upbeat here too. Many corporate, government, and UN funders and foundations generously contributed. The Chinese government agreed to provide the main logistical support in Beijing.

Then, things took a sharp turn for the worse. The Chinese organizers announced an abrupt change of venue that moved the location of the NGO Forum for Women away from the UN conference by a two-hour bus ride. The small town of Huairou, not Beijing, would host the world's women movement—a move designed to limit the numbers of participants and the possibility of mass demonstrations in the streets. I remember the shocked look on Supatra Masdit's face when she read the telegram from the All-China Women's Federation announcing the change. She turned pale. The Chinese delegate who had brought the message looked even more distressed.

• Weaving the World's Women in Beijing (1995)

A flurry of global NGO protests and campaigns followed that mobilized and demonstrated the force of the women's movement. Pressures on the UN and governments were persistent and widespread. Compromise was achieved.

On June 8, a new letter of agreement was signed. The Chinese organizers accepted a vastly increased number of participants, guaranteed a shuttle service and a satellite site near the UN conference center in Beijing. With barely two months left to organize the NGO Forum, we tossed out old maps and rushed to establish new ones. Hotel reservations changes and visas obstacles were only part of the confusion. It was clear to us that the real cost was being paid by the participants whose dreams were crumbling in a nightmare of logistics.

For the NGO Forum, the lives of organizers change completely. Sleep was what we did between crises, and insomnia took up the remaining time at night. What kept us going was the realization that thousands of women counted on us to stick together and work out problems with the Chinese organizers. All we had to do was keep a united front and hold the pieces together until the women of the world could arrive in Beijing to weave them together. So we did—and they did. Triumphantly.

Return to Huairou

At the time of the NGO Forum on Women in 1995, Huairou was a sleepy, provincial town on the outskirts of Beijing surrounded by peaceful low mountains and peach orchards. There were only two reasons Chinese visitors might stop in this town: a pleasant break on the way to the Great Wall or a very quiet spot for a leisurely weekend in the countryside. Few foreigners, if any, ever went there.

This all changed during the UN Fourth World Conference on Women when Huairou was chosen as the site of the NGO Forum. I was curious of how the people of Huairou feel about hosting the NGO Forum on Women and what at impact did the Conference have on the women. In search of answers, I made a return pilgrimage.

Leaving Beijing's traffic jams behind, I sighed with relief as we reached the wide-open roads leading to Huairou. In 1995, the locals had dubbed it the "women's superhighway." This was not a term of endearment so much as it was a reflection of reality. Heavy trucks and bicycles were banned at the time in order to leave the road free for the women's buses. As soon as the meeting ended, the Chinese quickly reclaimed it and transformed it into what I called "the super Yangtze."

Trucks carried their precious loads of fuel to the countryside. Bicycles headed into Beijing with every possible thing strapped on their frames: sleeping children, vegetables and watermelons—sometimes all at once.

At the border of Huairou County, our car passed under a red and white banner. Like a friendly Chinese fortune cookie, it read, "Welcome to tourism holiday spot of Huairou and expect everything to turn out as you wish." Banners are the Chinese way of bestowing good wishes on a special event and have an aura of old-fashioned good luck charms. Red in Chinese tradition symbolizes happiness and good fortune. For Huairou, it would forever have a distinct gender identity as well.

I stopped to buy some melons at a roadside stand. The couple running the stand were newlyweds who exemplified the new spirit of rural entrepreneurship. They had started this small business with only a tiny truck and a little cash. Our conversation soon strayed from melons to the NGO Forum on Women. They had been in Huairou when the women's conference took place.

"Did you see anything about it on television?" I asked. The young woman told me that they had watched, alongside everyone else. When I asked their thoughts on the results of the meeting, I expected a polite response about how it was a great event for China and how the people of Huairou were honored to have hosted the event. That kind of comment would tend to make the best impression in a political culture where personal opinions are rarely expressed to strangers. They didn't disappoint, telling me exactly what was expected. I continued my journey past billboards advertising an ostrich farm, cellular phones, and suburban housing developments.

The countryside just outside the town was filled with rows of red earthen and vinyl huts. I met briefly with Cai Tieying, the head of the March Eighth Women's Production Team, who explained that the agricultural co-op was founded and run entirely by women farmers.

The impact of the UN conference on the women of Huairou was

• Huairou NGO Forum entrance (1997)

local and global in more ways than one. Unbeknownst to the foreign visitors, village women had held their own parallel forums while the NGO Forum on Women was happening, so the collective spirit could include them. I imagined the women seated in the local community hall, discussing their recommendations for the Beijing Platform for Action. The successful March Eighth Women's Production Team was a direct outcome of their mini-NGO Forum workshop and an income-generating project.

"The Japanese gave us seeds for the cucumbers, and we export a lot of the produce abroad," Cai Tieying said. Organic vegetables were gaining popularity in Beijing, so the markets in big cities were also lucrative. I picked a sample and munched on the prickly cucumber, wondering if a Japanese homemaker in Tokyo and another in Beijing were doing the same thing.

A statue of a slim woman with her arms outstretched welcomed us to the center of town. I interpreted this gesture as welcoming, although it could easily have been seen by locals as a heavenly supplication to help survive the challenges of preparing for the hordes. Made of molded concrete, she had been hastily erected to commemorate a historic moment for women. At least the artists understood that what was happening to the town was more than just a sudden tourist boom.

I asked a police officer where the market that sold souvenirs, teapots, and quilts was. I thought I could easily do a few interviews there. The only problem was that it no longer existed. The police officer explained that everyone shopped at the big department store since 1995. On the other hand, he added that I could probably find what I wanted in a shopping mall next to the McDonald's sign.

I crossed the street to examine the Beijing-Huairou International Conference Center. Its large English sign stood out among the Chinese graphics as did the green dove suspended in the middle of its tall glass facade. This is the hall where Hillary Clinton had delivered her outspoken message on women's human rights. Over the doorway, a red banner now welcomed a meeting of international businesses to

Huairou. Like the rest of China, Huairou's internationalism has taken a distinctly commercial turn.

I saw crowds of students on bicycles nearby pour into the main street with a chatter that rose above the traffic noise. A group of young women stopped when the traffic policeman waved his arm, and they exchanged friendly words. Above their heads, I recognized the willow and evergreen trees. This place had been the heavily barricaded entrance to the NGO Forum. In 1995, heavy-handed, armed security guards prevented unwanted Chinese protesters from entering or even more importantly, radical women from marching out and demonstrating.

Farther up the road, at the Long Shan Hotel, I joined an international group of women for a briefing presented by the local representative of the All China Women's Federation. She said that hosting the NGO Forum was "a glorious time in the history of Huairou." Keeping in line with the development program approved by the state council, Huairou women mapped out their own county plan of action that focused on priorities such as poverty, women's literacy, health, and the environment. According to her report and confirmation from other sources, the government's financial input into Huairou was substantial, and women's programs grew immediately afterwards.

"During the campaign to promote nine years [of] compulsory education, we did a lot to ensure that all of the graduates of junior high school can enter senior high school," she said. "We also set up a special fund to aid children who live in poverty. In 1997, our health clinic for women and children was established and is now in operation. The statistics bureau is also doing a specific data collection to help promote the cause of women and children."

After the briefing, the vice mayor of Huairou hosted a lunch during which she explained that everything on the table was locally grown, including the ingredients for the ostrich curry and seasoned cucumbers. There was also a dish I didn't recognize.

"You are eating Mulan leaves," the vice mayor said. "I thought that since you are visiting the former site of the NGO Forum, this was an appropriate dish to serve." I recognized the name because I had just seen a preview of the movie based on the peasant girl, Mulan, who saved China from Mongolian invaders. Legends tell of how her Chinese troops were starving until she discovered that this wild mountain tree leaf was edible. We joked that if I ate these and went under the Huairou road banner, the combination might give me special powers. We finished the delicious meal and hoped for the best.

The vice mayor wished that Huairou would forever hold a special place in Chinese history. She wanted her town to become a center where the world's women could return and work together toward "women's liberation." To show their sincerity, the local women's committee proposed to build a monument to the world's women. This would be in the shape of a woman's hands with each finger a different color to symbolize the diversity of women working together. I thought it was a nice idea.

I hurried along the split path up the incline that led to the main grounds. The modern buildings that had once been used for the NGO Forum media center, newspaper site, and meeting rooms had been converted into a national sports training center. Large patches of urban gardens were flourishing on their grounds. Sunflowers rose high, and green beans were ready for picking. Behind one row I spotted three young women in their twenties. I asked if they had heard of the NGO Forum on Women.

"Oh yes, we were all volunteers there," one woman answered. "We served food in the main canteen." We exchanged memories. I told them that the women appreciated the friendly help of the young Chinese volunteers. They were impressed most by how women from so many different countries could be happy together in one place.

The small path extending past these gardens took me into the grounds where the large gray concrete meeting halls stood. I searched behind ruins and under fallen stones for some precious archeological evidence of a material culture left behind by the participants in the NGO Forum on Women. There wasn't a hairpin or pen to be found. I spotted a small broken sign and my hopes went up, but it turned out to be a military motto written by a team during a training session.

As soon as the women had left, these buildings were used for young men's boot camps. It was hardly the historic legacy I had expected, but I was pleased that almost everything else I'd seen suggested that the women of Huairou had actually gotten some direct benefit from the meeting three years ago. For me, that was something of a litmus test. If the NGO Forum had failed to produce some positive results for the local people who had made it happen, what hope was there for global progress? They passed my test.

The rain was getting heavier, so I headed back to the gate. Two old men standing near the gardens looked up and stared, wondering no doubt why I was shaking my feet so vigorously. My shoes were stuck in the famous Huairou mud. I smiled. I could almost hear the commotion of 30,000 women who had once gathered in the grounds behind me. Glancing back, I stepped off the sidewalk again into the mud on purpose, just to soak up more memories from the bottom of my feet.

Take Your Daughter to Vote

During the last presidential election in the United States, school children debated issues often with naive earnestness. One fifth grader said to me, "Well, I don't think past presidents kept their promises. Do you see a policeman on every corner?" I told her I didn't recall any promise of the sort, although I agreed that keeping campaign promises was important.

The next presidential election will be the central theme of many educational projects. Relying on paper voting booths and hand-cut campaign banners, children will aspire to imitate grown-up politics. Some will join the revelry of a mock convention and make wonderfully short-winded speeches. They will practice citizenship as if their futures depended on it. They will also be rewarded for good behavior in participatory politics. Apathy in this setting gets an F, not an A.

What happens between these years of imitation citizenry and real life? I wonder what can explain the average viewer's preference for mindless television to the serious business of choosing a mayor, senator or president.

Something is amiss. If the average citizen's dream is freedom from politics, this will soon be a reality. On average, less than 60 percent of American ever vote. If five percent were sick and another one percent was blown away by natural disasters, that still leaves a third of the eligible voting population in the "I don't feel like voting" category.

Compare this to elections in Thailand, South Africa, and Indonesia in the so-called "developing world." In these countries, more than 70 percent of voters show up at the polls. In comparison, America looks like a government of the elite few who get to the polls.

It is particularly worrisome that less than half of eligible women voters participated in presidential elections. Not that women always vote for feminist causes. In most countries, there is no guarantee that women will support women's rights. Raufa Hassan, a human rights activist who ran against conservative religious leaders in Yemen, got less than a third of women's votes. She found out the hard way that there is a feminist gap dividing women voters as well as a gender gap between women voters and men voters.

Nevertheless, demographic trends favor increasing women's influence in politics. In most industrialized countries, women voters now outnumber men. If women are well informed and willing to take the lead, they can make a major difference. For example, the League of Women Voters polls showed that in the 103rd United States Congress, women legislators voted for more family-friendly causes than did men. 91 percent of the women supported the ban on assault weapons, whereas only 66 percent of the men voted in favor of that measure (https://www.lwv.org).

Something has to compel women of diverse backgrounds, particularly young women, to jump into the voting pool. Maybe what is missing is the link between what happens in the classroom and what goes on at home. The practice of citizenship rights may need more attention from parents. Perhaps we have relied too much on teachers to drive home the meaning of the democratic creed; after all, they can only give students a taste of how democracy should work. The lessons learned at school have to be reinforced at home.

I propose we model a new campaign on the successful "take your daughter to work" program and start a movement to take our daughters to vote. We can show children how names are registered, how votes are tallied, and what mysteries lie behind the black curtain. For a son or a daughter, a childhood outing with a parent to vote could be the most important influence on their future political life. Then, classroom lessons would have meaning beyond an assignment and a family tradition that can be passed on to others.

Advice for a Worried Youth Leader

One day, I received a letter from a worried youth leader. She wrote:

Dear Soon-Young Yoon,

I have been invited to participate in the Generation Equality Forum to report on stories about young women and trafficking. I want to put my journalism training to good use, work from the human rights perspective, and get more involved with the UN. The problem is that I am not sure that I am qualified to be involved in global issues at the UN. Do I really belong in the company of all those ambassadors? Maybe you can suggest another young feminist who has kept up with international affairs. I even missed the 1995 Beijing women's conference. Please advise.

Sincerely yours,
Worried New Generation Leader

• Youth leaders at Habitat meeting in Indonesia (2020)

To her and many youth leaders like her, here is my advice about how to get involved with the UN:

1. **Don't give up.** These meetings should be for people just like you. We need global interactions between leaders and managers in civil society, not just reunions of professional conference attendees. The women's movement needs new blood.

2. **Complain more.** Youth groups are routinely trotted out for cultural performances, but they often are left out in the cold when it comes to getting on the speakers' list. Young women are often polite and don't say what is really on their mind. I know it's not easy. More veteran feminists may not take the time to help. However, if you don't get fair treatment, let the president of the official conference know that your problems are the UN's problems.

3. **Stick to what you know, but keep learning more.** What is often missing from these meetings is a heavy dose of reality. There will probably be a lot of statements about how governments have failed to keep their promises, but there also could be a shortage of good success stories. You are the best expert on your personal and community experiences. Learn more about your group's history, its leadership and financial situation, and make suggestions on how the UN, governments, businesses, and NGOs can better support youths.

4. **Know the UN political talk.** You don't have to agree with the UN to maneuver well in its midst. However, you do have to be well-armed with savvy lingo and expertise. On environment issues, I would start with the UN document, Agenda 21, which includes significant recommendations to solve global environment problems and positions related to gender inequality. For a little fun,

• Tanya Selvartnam. at the Youth tent (1995)

try quoting from commitments for the media made in the Beijing Platform for Action adopted in 1995. Since few finance ministers attended that meeting, most of them will probably be unaware of what these commitments were. Even women's groups are not well acquainted with what that document has to say about communications, information and the media.

5. **Learn the facts.** There are two steps you can take to become an instant expert on how to be effective at the UN. One is the NGO CSW/NY Advocacy training guide in negotiations and women's human rights at the UN. This is a good primer on the UN process as well as how feminist NGOs approved by ECOSOC can participate at the UN. Another is to read exten-

sively before you make statements so that you make them to the point and powerful.

6. **Remember that gender is a youth issue, too.** Join the women's caucus or women's major group meetings. An understanding of gender is absolutely crucial to grasping youth issues, particularly those dealing with sexual and reproductive health and human rights. Remember that you can be an expert without ever having heard about the UN conferences on women. Just trust your own experience and go from there.

7. **Young women's rights are human rights.** If you go on to pursue your concern for human rights, there is no better place than the UN to learn and act. These days, we need to have more young people involved. Many of the international treaties that could be used to protect your rights are seldom used. For example, violence against women is often directed at girls. Like adult women, young women can also claim their right to protection against all forms of sexual, mental, and physical violence by referring to international covenants. Young women's human rights issues—sexual violence, rape, sexual torture, forced pregnancy, and domestic violence—should all be highlighted at youth assemblies. Similarly, it is important to call on governments to protect those rights through legislation and social services.

8. **Be proud, but not too full of yourself.** Remember that after years of activism, you are very qualified to join an eminent group of organizers and leaders. Carry your issues up to a global level and bring them to the attention of heads of state. Don't give up so soon.

A New Phoenix Rises

In the inner court of Beijing's Forbidden City, a carving of the mythical phoenix decorates the outer wall of the empress's palace like a talisman to ward off evil spirits. The phoenix was the court's favorite symbol of the empresses' power. According to legend, the phoenix died in a fiery death only to rise from the ashes of its own destruction. No wonder empresses held the phoenix dear. They probably thought that heaven guaranteed them immortal powers.

I think there is a modern variation of the traditional phoenix symbol. Like the mythical bird, Chinese women have had their historical moments, wielding power and then vanishing from sight. Yet in each era, their political spirit was reborn, usually with a different identity.

This century is a propitious time for a new Chinese phoenix to rise. Ideological certainties are being re-examined, and serious cracks have developed in the plan for paradise on earth. In China, as in many other one-time communist strongholds, things didn't turn out quite as expected. Today, isolationism, big government, and central planning are unpopular artifacts, replaced by internationalism, private enterprise, and free markets.

Amidst this transition, Chinese women needed only a brief opportunity to become the center of national attention. The Fourth World Conference on Women provided that chance. According to scholars at Beijing University, the most immediate result of the Conference was a great leap forward in women's political participation.

In the 1990s, Wu Qing, a distinguished professor of American studies at the Chinese International University, was a leading evangelist for the cause. Toting a grassroots political philosophy, she traveled around the country, speaking to communities and women's groups. Her main message was that women must exercise their rights by voting and holding their local representatives accountable. Wu believed that the future of women's political power lay in mobilizing their political consciousness and encouraging more independent-minded women to run for office. That kind of conviction was hard to beat.

Wu spoke from her own experience as a successful independent candidate for the prestigious People's Congress. In her spare time, she opened her university office to her constituency to stay in touch with their concerns. They told her everything, from family problems to illnesses, and she listened. Her views may have strayed from the party line, but she insisted that everything she espoused was legal.

The Conference also marked a turning point for the largest women's non-governmental organization in the world: The All China Women's Federation (ACWF). There were stable financial resources that strengthened its political clout. Thanks to the visibility of the Conference, the ACWF had considerable backing from the government and international donors to provide services needed by Chinese women. The ACWF launched popular anti-poverty and literacy campaigns that reached millions of women. Its departments included human resources development, publicity and education, children's work, and international liaison. A publishing house, several magazines, and the *China Women's Daily* were also affiliated. These social services, combined with strong media outreach, guaranteed that the ACWF was a major player in the country's struggle for social and economic reform.

The Conference didn't turn China upside down by itself, but it clearly contributed to the country's political renaissance. Above all, it helped to encourage many Chinese women to see themselves as leaders at the forefront of China's modernization. Striving to be assertive and demanding self-respect, young women in particular are making progress toward power. They are challenging traditional authoritarian models of centralized power and heavy-handed rule. For the new leaders of the Chinese women's movement, the imperial manner of authoritarian leadership is part of the old order.

The feminization of politics in China has taken on a new purpose: encouraging women's equal participation and leadership in a democratic society. The phoenix has risen. May it grow strong and fly higher.

From Victims to Visionaries

Nearly a quarter century after the international women's movement swept through Huairou, China, at the NGO Forum in 1995, we are still pondering the magnitude and meaning of the event. Many women experienced a kind of magic that changed their lives. In the crowds, no one was a stranger. A young student from New York joined hands with a villager from El Salvador and a Chinese painter. They could not speak each other's language, but they danced together in the Healing Tent of the NGO Forum. Who would have thought that the hokey pokey dance could be a ritual dance of empowerment?

Veterans of the first UN World Conference on Women in Mexico City (1975) could see that something was different about this UN meeting. In the eyes of some women leaders, the international women's movement had grown-up. As one Latin American feminist put it, "Women no longer saw themselves as downtrodden victims." Instead, they were celebrating their power and claiming their rights as citizens. The tactics had changed from confrontation as the only and main strategy to the use of mass media and successful lobbying. The result of the Conference was a new self-image: examining equality, develop-

• Latin American women protest in Mar del Plata (1994)

ment, and peace from women's perspectives, not just as women's problems.

"It was not a world conference about women, but a women's conference about the world," said Noeleen Heyzer, former director of UNIFEM (now UN Women).

In the eyes of many participants, all issues were women's issues. Women want to redefine the structures, cultures, and values of development. The regional NGO Forum documents not only recorded women's perspectives on health, education, and welfare, but also the development topics of international banking, structural adjustment, the environment, and international affairs.

Since the 1970s, women activists have argued that most UN and government agencies based their early development policies on a false image of women and children as passive, helpless victims of social injustice. Report after report of unequal status in education, health, and economic status reinforced this view. The state was a patriarchal father whose duty was to look after its dependents of women and children. However, the diagnosis of social ills was always incomplete be-

• Arab states regional meeting with Palestinean leaders (2014)

cause of inaccurate information and incomplete data.

The picture became clearer in the 1980s as UN and national statistics confirmed the role of women as major contributors to every country's gross national product as workers and economic decision-makers. While development models recast their programs to fit a new image, the international women's movement became increasingly uncomfortable with their role as victims.

A world conference shines the spotlight on a global consensus whose strength had been building before and continues after the event. The NGO Forum in 1995 was that special moment in history when visions for good were clear and the fog of ignorance was lifted. Years later at regional meetings and at the UN Commission on the Status of Women, the vision has evolved to make sure that we build unity with diversity. More than ever the "intersectionality" or multiple layers of discrimination born by women is part of the feminist framework. This concept includes migrant and refugee women, indigenous women and girls, those living with disabilities, non-binary people, and those facing racism as well as discrimination by ethnicity, religion, political, economic and social status.

Through the UN women's conferences, and the international movements they launched, the feminist and women's movements experienced a gradual and intentional transformation of their collective identity. Women would no longer be passive bystanders to be rescued as victims, but active participants in finding solutions to the world's problems. Our role was not only to uplift ourselves, but to share our dreams for equality, development, and peace with the rest of the world.

Is Patriarchy Fragile?

The stereotype of Korea's pre-modern history is that it was steeped in Confucianism. A preference for boys was a common reason for women to have more children because according to traditional law, only male heads of household were allowed to conduct ancestral rites. If everyone followed these patriarchal rules, then where did the Korean spirit of women's revolt come from? How did women during Japanese occupation in the 1930s rise up as leaders of the anti-colonial movement? What explains the central role that strong-willed rural women leaders played in South Korea's economic boom?

It turns out that patriarchal culture is much more fragile than we think. Beneath the veneer of patriarchal cultures lie cultures of resistance. Wherever men had power, women also created their own spaces of respect and influence. Anthropologists understand that cultures are very heterogenous and full of contradictions. That is how in the most dominant patriarchal cultures, we often find optimal breeding grounds for a powerful women's movement.

In a sense, powerful women living in a patriarchal society are also part of traditional Korean culture. The mother-in-law has been a

• Adama Diop and I are at the Women's March in New York (2018)

strong political figure in the household, acting as the traditional midwife and holding the family purse strings.

However, strong women who exert influence in male-dominated societies are everywhere. As a UNICEF officer, I visited villages and poor urban communities in Indonesia, Thailand, Burkina Faso, France, Senegal, and India. In these and other countries known to have national laws that discriminate against women, I found that local women are often opinion leaders and custodians of modern as well as customary religious practices.

Blaming culture for women's oppression is problematic in societies where women are the culture bearers and the main strongholds of a community's cultural identity. Myrna Cunningham Kain, former chair of the UN Indigenous Peoples' Forum, defends culture as a development asset. At various UN FORA, she has called for the UN to recognize and respect the cultural heritage and identity of rural women.

I'm concerned that too many recent UN reports about cultural norms categorically portray culture as a barrier to women's empowerment and full participation. Here is one example: "Cultural norms, care responsibilities, and security issues mean that women and girls face more difficulties than their male counterparts in gaining access to local and national markets and institutions" (E/CN.6/2012/3 p, 17).

It is true that traditions like female genital mutilation are perpetuated in the guise of respect for cultural traditions. It is also wrong for governments to hide behind culture as an excuse to be complacent about reforming discriminatory family laws that violate women's rights. At the same time, the oversimplification of culture as a problem does not advance our understanding of women's personal and collective resources. As a matter of accuracy, we should distinguish between harmful cultural norms and those that empower women.

If women have one lesson to teach about social change, it is this: where there has been a culture of oppression, there have always been custodians of hope. You only have to find them and let them speak.

Winners of the Campaign for Change

American presidential campaigns are archetypes of modern-age politics. Orchestrated mostly at the top by professionals, campaigns invested millions of dollars on focus groups to craft messages, publicity, television appearances, and image makeovers. The complexities of political platforms are simplified and streamlined, then tailored to reach target audiences. The political economies of these campaigns are undeniably robust. Given the extraordinary resources at their command, you wonder how either party could ever lose.

For leaders in the international women's movement, this high-flying style seems far beyond reach. While women should always aim high, we should be thankful that not everyone believes that big budgets are the only way to win public support. Some activists have successfully gone mainstream, cutting into the mass-media power line and accessing big-time money. For the rest of us, candlelight vigils, testimonials, and white ribbons are as extravagant as we get. The surprising result is that these low-cost alternative strategies are both cheaper and often leave a more enduring impression.

One telling example is the 16 Days of Activism Against Gender

Violence campaign, which ends on Human Rights Day on December 10. The campaign positively thrives on volunteers and limited resources. By its 20th anniversary in 2020, the campaign had grown into a global phenomenon. Years ago, under the leadership of Charlotte Bunch, founder of the Center for Women's Global Leadership, a handful of women dreamed of global mobilization that would push governments into action to curb violence against women. Today, many governments have made the Campaign a national celebration. UN Women participates in the campaign, so some people even mistakenly think that it is an official UN-sponsored event.

The campaign has developed a novel political strategy based on unity with diversity. The Center sets the theme, such as ending gender-based violence in the world of work. However, everyone decides their own priorities within these themes. One year, American Feminists for Animal Rights planned workshops showing the connection between violence against women and violence against animals. The Spanish Men's Group Against Male Violence held a meeting called "Towards a New Masculinity." Women's groups in Argentina organized a concert with singers protesting violence. Art projects in Ireland displayed 200 tiles with women's names written on them. White ribbon events were planned in Cambodia, Australia, India, Spain, and England.

These events all took place without a central office orchestrating messages and planning strategies. The key has been to unite all events on a single calendar, giving all those who participate the exhilarating sense of a global, collective effort. The Center invites all participants to send their plans for the campaign. Daily calendars are posted on a website, and groups can share contact points and information. The entire campaign has an amazingly coherent impact.

There is another important impact of such campaigns. Rather than leaving the public feeling like they had been sold political products and targeted for even more, the campaign empowers those who participate. It provides a collective space for feminist and women's groups that might otherwise feel alone in their efforts to take up sensitive issues, like violence against women. Of course, partisan millionaire donors are not likely to finance this campaign. However, women can achieve personal as well as political victories by changing their own course and by going their own way.

If You Don't Vote, We Will

One day during an American presidential election, I received an urgent phone call from the prime minister of a tiny South Asian island. She had been following the campaign closely and was very agitated.

"I heard that less than half of the eligible voters were going to the polls," she exclaimed. She wanted to know if there had been a military coup or threats of terrorist attacks or if women were being threatened if they went to the polls. I tried to dispel her fears about terrorist threats and answered that I hadn't seen any tanks in the streets, but I couldn't explain why so few Americans show up to vote. Although there were hundreds of polls conducted during the campaign, few of them, if any, had asked Americans why they weren't voting. The media's explanation was that the public generally saw one candidate as stiff and the other as dull and that alone was enough for voters to tune out of an election.

A friend of mine has a less charitable explanation. He worried that the American presidential elections have become a spectator sport that voters watch from a distance, akin to watching a winner emerge from the World Series. In his opinion, Americans love to see an exciting battle of champions, whether in politics or sports. However, if candidates don't rise to the level of stardom, even party loyalists might show their disdain by boycotting the polls and turning to more engaging local. He pointed out that the real tragedy is that the political game is not a contest between people, but teams. For example, casting a vote for a conservative candidate is a vote for an entire phalanx of ultra conservatives.

The prime minister was impatient with my attempts to explain.

"In our country," she said, "everyone knows the candidates and their positions on issues, like abortion, foreign aid, and the environment. We watch American elections as much as our own because the outcome of these elections is critical to our future. If American policy on global warming doesn't get on track, the sea level is going to rise, and half of our country will sink beneath the waves. Our maternal child healthcare services are improving with the help of American foreign aid, but if the anti-abortion conservatives win, our women will no longer have the right to reproductive choice. Don't Americans understand that their president is a world leader too?"

I couldn't calm her down. At this point, she made a daring proposal. She was going to write a letter to the new president offering to fill the gap in the American political structure. The note would say:

> "Your people do not seem to be enthusiastic about voting for presidents. We can only surmise that the citizens who stay at home are happy to let strangers determine who will lead the country. As strangers go, we are actually the most qualified. Why? Because we have keenly studied the candidates' qualifications, the issues, and weighed the consequences on the world. Therefore, we propose that if Americans won't vote, we will. If you grant us this privilege, we promise to make informed decisions and take full responsibility to help bear the burden of democracy."

I marveled at her imagination and her earnest desire to enhance the democratic process. At the end of the day, those of us in major democratic states need to be to remind the public that if they don't choose their leaders, someone else will. I cast my vote to have my friend from the tiny South Asian island appear on primetime television and make her offer to join the electoral process. It's a message worth hearing for all future elections everywhere.

Where are the Men?

The gender count of participants at UN conferences has been a sore point for decades. Mildred Persinger, former president of the International Women's Tribune Center, remembered the Bucharest population summit in 1974 as an event that changed her life.

"All of the men were deciding what women should do about contraception, abortion, and family planning," she said. The next year, he was equally upset that most heads of delegations at the 1975 World Conference on Women, including the president of the conference, were men. Ever since, she had been vigilant about asking UN organizers where the women were.

According to a UN Women report decades later, the same question was still being asked. By 2018, the number of women in executive government positions had stagnated. The private sector—usually the hub of innovative governance—also falls short. Among multinational corporations and bank boards of governors, there are only a few women CEOs and chairs.

Recently at the UN Commission on the Status of Women meetings, women were asking a different question: Where are the men?

Arab regional meeting in Amman (1994)

Over the years, women have been so effective in raising political awareness about equal representation that the majority of the 4,000 delegates annually were women. Yet something was amiss. Some women wondered if any men had even heard about the women's conferences. With four major summits behind them, it was beginning to look like women were preaching to the converted. It was time to make more men take responsibility for women's rights. After all, references to men's responsibilities for promoting gender equality have started to appear in more and more final documents.

These women were right on track, but the solution is not so simple. The gender imbalance in UN conferences reflects much deeper problems at home. At the ministerial level, Sweden is the one of the few countries that has had as many female as male ministers. Few countries have appointed men as gender ministers, recognizing that men's leadership roles are critical to achieve gender equality. The issue of women's empowerment remains largely absent from the agenda of most meetings in the public and private sectors.

A breakthrough of governments occurred during the UN Climate

Change negotiations. With the help of Mary Robinson, former President of Ireland, women's organizations lobbied governments to pass the first gender-balance resolution in a UN treaty. These organizations included the Women's Environment and Development Organization (WEDO). The agreement called for annual reports on the numbers of women and men serving on government negotiations teams. In 2017, a gender plan was also sketched out to help ensure that gender equality and women's empowerment in climate change moved higher on the list of political priorities. If words turn into action, the gender balance sheet of the UN meetings should look better in the future. We must keep on counting until the answers no longer matter.

What the UN Fourth World Conference on Women Achieved

The final tally of the Beijing women's conference's achievements was very impressive. Here are some headlines. Governments supporting the Holy See were unable to derail the strong language that supported sexual and reproductive health and rights. Some states finally adopted the NGO amendments with reservations, a diplomatic way of saying that they agreed but disagreed. Issues about the girl-child, violence against women, and structural adjustment were given adequate attention, thus forging stronger commitments to the 12 Critical Areas of Concern, a set of priorities identified as most likely to contribute in the short-term to women's equality.

The international women's movement asserted its right to speak on all issues as women's issues. Women wanted to redefine the structures, culture, and values of development, and they no longer saw themselves as victims. Instead, they established their rights as citizens. It was a matter of looking at the world through women's eyes.

There was a search for greater commonality between women in rich and poor countries to work together. Together, they acknowledged that solutions to global poverty, environmental degradation,

• Opening ceremonies in Beijing (1995)

negative impact of the media, and new information technologies involve everyone. The rich nations of the North recognized that they too were made up of immigrant, poor, and disenfranchised groups.

At the UN conference, delegates recognized that the true enemy of peace was not war between nations, but an absence of a culture of peace. Before there can be a lasting peace between nations, there must be an enduring peace in family life. There cannot be an end to global ethnic violence while domestic violence persists. There cannot be a moral separation between private and public spheres. Responsibility for domestic violence was no longer a private issue, but now a public, legal issue.

Since the International Conference on Population and Development (ICPD) in Cairo in 1994, the concept of women's health has been closely tied to women's empowerment and education. Emphasis was appropriately given to health information and prevention, such for HIV/AIDS. Health services should deal with women's complete

• Women's event in Beijing (1995)

state of well-being, mental and physical, throughout the life cycle and address the needs of girls, adolescents, and the aged.

Human rights emerged as a new moral instrument for women's rights. It stood for more than political and civil rights and applied to the wide range of development issues, such as women's health, education, media, and economics.

Gender as a social construct of the relationships between men and women was debated and entered into the Beijing Platform for Action (BPfA). This controversial concept affirmed that "biology is not destiny." There are social and cultural differences that define gender inequality.

We could also count the paragraphs included. We should be proud of gains made, but the most important achievements of the BPfA are invisible. Even if governments go home and go about business as usual, the women's movement has the potential to carry this document and make governments accountable through voting. Furthermore, this constituency is now better organized and more global than ever before. The mobilization around the BPfA and the Fourth World Conference on Women strengthened the NGO network in a spider web-like structure from grassroots to regional levels. Leadership diversified, and regional, subregional, national and subnational structures emerged with working groups and issue caucuses. These spider web-like structures continued to evolve and held on long after the conference in Beijing was over.

UN Airlines to the Future

Ladies and gentlemen, welcome aboard United Nations Air flight number A/CONF.177/20—your bargain shuttle to the Fifth World Conference on Women. We urgently request a doctor to cure some delegates showing signs of brain damage. There are a few dizzy spells lingering from stalled discussions during the last preparatory meeting in New York on key subjects concerning women's sexual and reproductive health and rights. Our preliminary diagnosis is that this is hypochondria, a fake illness that is likely to reappear in all future meetings. The Women's Caucus suggests that these delegates stay in bed, so they can read previous agreements. Delegates who negotiated at the International Conference on Population and Development are fit to travel to this global gathering.

We apologize for any translation problems on this flight. Due to budget cuts, our flight attendants no longer receive language training. However, we have tried to accommodate these differences with multilingual personnel. Your cabin crew today includes a few former government officials who have volunteered for this flight in lieu of their country's contribution to the UN. Let's give them a hand.

We understand that although some non-governmental organizations (NGOs), women's groups, and journalists pushed the emergency button several times during previous meetings, most countries declined to be alarmed. Looking at the state of our world, some observers think drastic action is the only rational response. However, we commend you for your reasonable and cautious attitude and have seated those troublemakers in the rear of the plane. Those NGOs who tried to take seats in first class and chat up the folks with real power are being appropriately disciplined. We regret that they often try to gain access to areas that are off limits. They will not be given the final UN document or earphones for entertainment.

In the interest of environmental consciousness, we are happy to announce that there will be no food or beverage service during this flight. The wasted food, plastic utensils, and trays will not be a black spot on our waste disposal record. We couldn't afford all those frills anyway. Please try to cooperate with our new procedures. At this time, the captain has turned on the "no smoking" sign. In keeping with the concern for the environment, we hope you will put up similar signs in all lavatories and public places in your countries.

In the front seat pocket, there are changes proposed for the document that were not taken seriously at the regional preparatory meetings. These changes represent the statements compiled by the NGO International Facilitating Committee and the Women's Caucus. If you are unable to finish reading these during the flight, you are invited to take your complimentary copies to the meeting, where they belong anyway.

Those of you who are frequent fliers on our UN Air conference flights will earn an additional 1,500 pages of documents points for your outstanding performance on the UN reading test. Many of you have been to so many UN meetings that you have already reached the Gold Elite category. This allows you to upgrade your seats to the cockpit, where you can discuss issues with the new woman Secretary General, who is the pilot for this flight.

Congratulations to NGOs, architects, and governments for some excellent recommendations on how to improve human settlements during the Habitat IV meeting. To the left of the plane, you can see the model urban settlements built in two weeks according to the guidelines drawn up at the conference. It was a rush job in order to have them ready for the photographers. If you do not recognize your recommendations, we suggest you consult with local contractors and city officials about what happened to them.

We thank you for flying with us today. As you know, this is a new privatized venture for the UN. It is the wave of the future. Since we can't get government funding, we have no choice. In keeping with our newfound faith in the market economy to solve every problem, UN Air is funded almost entirely by passenger patronage, interest from the UN pension fund, and change contributed to the charity box at the airport. We expect to expand our routing and upgrade our DC-3s. Remember our motto: "We're all in this together, so fly UN Air to the next century."

The Ghost of Conferences Past

On the last day of the Beijing Plus Five meeting in New York, I saw a ghostly figure handing out leaflets. Dressed in a gray jacket and long skirt, this young woman looked oddly old-fashioned. My curiosity was aroused.

"Hi," I said. "What organization do you represent?"

To my surprise, she answered. "I belong to the youth caucus and I am here to make sure that none of the previous agreements made at other UN meetings are changed," she said as she handed me a leaflet that was blank except for a large black comma drawn on it. "Our group does not believe that this comma belongs where the delegate from Grenada put it, and we are here to set the record straight. In the document agreed upon in 1995, that comma was definitely before, and not after, the word 'equal.'"

Suddenly I was paying attention. Here was a lobbyist so faithful to the text that she had even memorized the punctuation. She believed that a UN document was like a bible that must never change, so she was relentless in her mission.

Then a cloud of pessimism passed over me. "What difference

would that make?" I asked myself. Did the future of women's equal rights hang on this grammatical change? The young woman saw my puzzled expression and began a tiresome lecture on the importance of being faithful to previous agreements. I cut her short by saying that I would catch her later.

On reflection, I confess that her point of view was consistent with the mantra, "Don't Slide Back." Nevertheless, I cringed at the possibility that future meetings would get bogged down by commas. Moreover, I regretted that youth groups were so blindly drawn into lobbying about words rather than actions that they couldn't see past the grammar. When I saw her the next day, I argued with her, "You are right to defend the original agreements, but we also have to enlarge our vision and update our approach. We can use the agreements made in the past as a foundation, but we have to understand them in the bright colors of the present. We must see their possibility to light the way to the future."

"The Platform for Action is only a wonderful floor, not the ceiling of possibilities," I continued. "Many years later, we can restack our priorities in action coalitions. Women's sexual and reproductive health and rights have been placed squarely at the center of sustainable development. Other issues like climate change, health, globalization, science and technology need more attention." She just stared at me, handed me another leaflet and walked away like a gloomy shadow.

No one else caught a glimpse of her. She could become invisible. To avoid this, we must revive the spirit of the Beijing conference. The energy and vision of the international women's movement has been nurtured by energized, creative new thinkers who are testing its strength on the ground. We need to point our youth in a more productive, forward direction that could breathe life into the feminist and women's movement at the UN once again.

The Commission on the Status of Women

If you don't know what CSW stands for, you can join 95 percent of the world's women. I first learned of the UN CSW in 1980, when I worked with the UN Secretariat for the second UN World Conference on Women. I was a novice in the Secretariat and had to catch up on endless UN acronyms. To the outside world, CSW could stand for almost anything. Combat Submission Wrestling or Certified Specialist of Wine came to mind.

I soon learned that CSW stood for the Commission on the Status of Women. The CSW was founded in 1946, only one year after the UN's creation, and is the oldest of six UN commissions. It was created to promote the principle of equal rights for men and women. Specifically, it oversees the progress of legally binding treaties, such as the Convention on the Elimination of All Forms of Discrimination against Women (CEDAW), and works with UN Women, the main UN body responsible for implementing programs for gender equality and women's empowerment.

At a high level, the CSW is meant to be a catalyst to ensure that the UN and world governments live up to their promises to women

• NGO march during CSW in New York (2012)

for equality, development, and peace. It has to do a review and assessment of progress in implementation of the Beijing Platform for Action, including the all-important albeit unglamorous provision on institutional mechanisms for the advancement of women, including all of the ministries of gender and women's affairs.

That's a tall order. However, the CSW has never shied away from the challenges of responding to the international women's movement's demands for change while upholding intergovernmental and UN rules. The legacy of the CSW goes back to the international women's movement and human rights movements in the 1930s that eventually led to the UN's founding in 1945. The CSW steered the process for the UN world women's conferences in Mexico (1975), Copenhagen (1980), Nairobi (1990), and Beijing (1995).

Innovation has to come from somewhere within the UN. I believe the CSW is a shining example of how to build a strong international organization that ensures that governments, social movements, and the UN come together to defend women's human rights. However, the CSW will simply rehash old ideas if we don't take the responsibility to set it on the right course. The annual CSW meeting is an excellent opportunity to make sure that creative ideas flourish. NGOs gathered at that event will have a chance to speak out on how the UN's sustainable development goals on peace and security, climate change, and science and technology can support gender equality and women's empowerment.

What can you contribute to the CSW session next year?

Chapter 8

Circle of Women: Portraits

"Smart people have their heads bowed low because there is so much wisdom in them."

_ Song Kyung-Shyn

Introduction

The women in this chapter have inspired me by their courage, faith in humanity, and joy in helping others. Each one contributes a spark of hope to the women's movement. While many elected politicians jostle for fame and seek rewards, these women have carried out social and political struggles with humility and grace. Each one has had an impact that have improved people's lives far beyond their imaginations. Some heroines, like Song Pok-Shyn, my aunt, and Mun Ok-Sun, the shaman, inspired others through their life stories. Although these women are no longer with us, I have tried to capture the essence of their legacy. Other women in this chapter still have tales to tell. I invite you to know them better.

Mama Mongella

As a public figure, Gertrude Mongella is best known as a minister, ambassador, and former Secretary General of the Fourth World Conference on Women. Nevertheless, I always preferred the honorable rank her African sisters gave her: Mama Mongella. This title showed their respect and affection. Although she is quick to smile and give a reassuring embrace, she also carries a big stick when things need to get done. Like a traditional African queen mother, she knows how to use her authority to impose the law. Mama Mongella is no one to be trifled with.

After she left the UN, she travelled a dizzying course across the globe. Airplanes became her favored vacation spots. Up in the air, she took off her shoes, read a magazine, and forgot that she was on her way to another quick stop on her journey for world peace. There was time to prepare her speeches, which were known for their impromptu, off-the-cuff humor. Some of the tough words also got sugar coatings. Once a school teacher, she has never forgotten that if you want to make students remember the lesson, you have to get straight to the point through a well-rounded tale.

• On the road with Mama Mongella (1994)

I have always been amused and impressed by her originality. Her slow, deliberate manner hides a quick mind that picked up every body language signal, from a friendly tone of voice or a mean glint in the eye. She sizes up new experiences and rolls the tough ones over in her mind like a boulder until they are reduced to pebbles under her feet. She constantly updates her political handbook.

She believed that after a UN women's conference ended, everyone should go home to do their homework. When I asked her about her priorities, she didn't hesitate. Peace was at the top of the list. She told me that African governments agreed with her suggestions for social development, such as improving girls' education and women's health. However, the next time she visited those countries, they were often fighting. That is when she realized that unless the African continent is free from conflict, the Beijing Platform for Action can never be implemented.

"This peace question gets me angry," she said. "I'm angry toward our leaders for spending money on arms. How can the international community send arms to Africa and ignore it? It is immoral to go to a poor man's door and sell poison. We can work to stop the landmines and to prevent ships carrying arms from leaving harbor or anchoring. If we manage that, it will be a signal to the world that women are networking together."

Although she doesn't hesitate to lash out at African men, she does it like a wife angry at a husband for getting the family into trouble. "Men are largely to blame," she said, "but women are partly responsible for talking too much to themselves. We women are becoming better, faster thinking in human rights and economic issues than men. We have had a lot of time to analyze these in our conferences. Some men haven't had that chance, so we are creating the men of yesterday, whereas we are the women of tomorrow." Her solution is to bring more men to women's meetings and involve them more in negotiations about women's rights.

Another issue close to her heart is women's political empowerment. Again, she doesn't let women off the hook. She doesn't think women have taken advantage of the political clout they already have. "The vote is the only weapon a poor peasant or woman has. Take government representatives out of their seats, and if they know that you plan to do that, they are going to respect you. If you put in a conservative government, you can put that government out," she said.

We must understand that women could gain a great deal just by exercising the right to vote. Women should also be more willing to take chances, to contend for political offices, and to run for the presidency. Mama Mongella certainly thinks these are worthy goals. That's what I like most about her. She doesn't just aim high. She never doubts that success is possible.

Noeleen Heyzer

Plato longed for a philosopher-ruler who would use knowledge and wisdom to create an ideal society, but he would have been astounded that a Malaysian woman of Dutch lineage would aspire to be such a leader. Noeleen Heyzer, director of the United Nations Development Fund for Women (UNIFEM, now UN Women), has high standards that would suit his ideal type, and she planned to make sure the UN had them too.

When I first met Heyzer, she was a postgraduate fellow at the Institute for Development Studies in Sussex, England. Between classes, we exchanged ideas about working motherhood, women's welfare, and research. I asked daily about her twins, who were dropped off at the school daycare center. Even then, she would break into her trademark smile at the oddest moments, just like when she spoke about how difficult the pregnancy had been. I quickly guessed her secret to survival: when disaster strikes, find the silver linings and turn them into shining armor.

Here is her story. She was born in a remote Malay village during the British colonial era, and her mother died when she was only six.

• Noeleen Heyzer

Her grandmother had to raise her in one of the poorest areas of Singapore. Most of her childhood neighbors were poverty-stricken and marginalized. She learned of other children's misfortunes from her aunt, who ran a Catholic orphanage. It was a haven for children born just before the Year of the Tiger started. They were abandoned because their families believed that such children would eat the parents.

Heyzer said that living among such unfortunate people was a good experience because she grew up exposed to different class and ethnic situations. Fortunately, she was also enrolled at an elite school for diplomats' children. Although she attended several different Catholic schools, the teachers were mostly foreign men who were dedicated to creating a new generation of women leaders for an independent Singapore. In the 1960s, when Singapore gained its formal independence, she was in secondary school, getting more than her share of intellectual molding in philosophy, humanities, and political thought.

As challenging as her life had been, Heyzer did not feel that fate had given her a raw deal. That would betray a lack of faith in human destiny—something she would never admit. When asked about her experiences with French Jesuit priests, she said, "The one thing I learned in secondary school was that a leader doesn't mean that you snatch power. Leadership at the end of the day is service. That also means you have the capacity to do extraordinary things well. You don't grab power. It is given to you." A star pupil, she probably found that when she proved she could get things done, others followed.

While a university student, Heyzer wanted to know more about how ordinary workers lived. After graduating, she took a job as a textile worker—an experience that changed how she looked at her own leadership role. She had been tutored to believe that great leaders did not dabble in women's issues, but rather with the important ones like international relations and public policy. During her factory days, she did not question the validity of such notions. As the international secretary of the Democratic Socialist Club, she traveled abroad and mingled with the European intellectual elite, discussing the future of Asian geopolitics and economic development. However, the experience of working with factory girls moved her so much that she learned to see the world through their eyes and remodeled her own life accordingly to champion women's causes.

Her first high-paying job was in a bank, but that interest faded as quickly as the clink of a cash register. When she returned to graduate school at Cambridge, her desire to study propelled her into gender studies, economic development, and international relations. After several years working in the Social Development division of the Economic and Social Commission for Asia and Pacific in Thailand, she joined UNIFEM. She found the office in the midst of crisis. With sheer determination, she took the opportunity to reorganize its programs. In typical, efficient fashion, she removed bureaucratic cliques, heroically redesigned the budget, and streamlined the organization.

Heyzer would like to see her efforts at the UN contribute to the elimination all forms of violence—physical, mental, economic and military—against women. She felt that violence against women was the major impediment to all future development. That theme resonated years later in the sustainable development goals and remains true to this day.

Mun Ok-Sun

I met Mun Ok-Sun on my first trip to Jeju Island. We could hardly communicate because she spoke the Jeju dialect, and I was—as she put it—"deaf and dumb" as far as Korean was concerned. Standing a little shorter than me, we literally saw eye to eye on how important it was to help poor rural women.

She was a former diver who became "possessed" by a spirit after her husband was killed by Japanese soldiers during the colonial occupation. She had been active in the anti-colonial movement, but she had a hard life when peace was restored. Over the years, her reputation grew so that in her 60s, she became one of the grandest shamans. Jeju shamans are organized into a hierarchy with fortune-tellers at the bottom and "kun shimbang" shamans at the top. She was one of the latter. Mun adopted me as her spiritual daughter and invited me to follow her team of four shamans from one ceremony (called a "kut") to another. Sometimes, my job was to play the cymbals.

She conducted many ceremonies to treat ailments that involved psychosomatic symptoms. One of the most memorable was a healing ceremony for a woman who couldn't speak. A young daughter-in-law

Mun Ok-Sun prepares for a shaman ceremony

was brought in with an affliction that was clearly mental as well as physical. because she would moan, "aiiiigu" to express her pain. Nothing was wrong with her lungs or throat. Yet, try as they might, her in-laws and husband could not get her to voice even the simplest complaint in words. For all practical purposes, she was essentially mute. The onset of her problem coincided with a fight she had with her mother-in-law, who was now distressed and feeling guilty about having caused such trauma.

For the cure, Mun summoned all of the ancestors to the family's home from both the wife and husband's side. For nearly three days, food, drink, dancing, and ceremonies were presented to the ancient spirits to please them and bring them down to earth. Exorcisms were performed in gentle strokes of rice paper on the patient's back, and the clang-clang of the brass cymbals helped attract the attention of neighbors and family to her plight. Then, on the last day, the shaman coaxed the exhausted patient to respond in words to her spirits' call.

The work of the ancestors had been completed. More care and attention to a poor daughter-in-law also helped.

In another case involving a tuberculosis patient, I watched Mun use a different approach. A man had stopped taking his medicine and now too weak to work, had begun drinking. Neither doctors nor his wife could convince him to give up alcohol or resume taking his medications. He wanted to escape it all, and the shamans had to find a way to bring him back to reality. In one segment of the ceremony, Mun suddenly shook and began to speak in the voice of the TB patient's dead father. Speaking through her, the ghost spoke of how the man's sisters had died because they didn't receive as much food or clothing as the boys. The girls' spirits were now hungry and unhappy.

According to Mun, that was one reason for the man's illness. Then, she turned into the patient's mother, who spoke about how she suffered after her husband's death. There was ritual weeping and wailing. I sped up the rhythm of my clanging to keep up with the drum. The moment was tense. Finally, Mun jumped up and down quickly at a quicker pace. Dropping down on her hands and knees, she bowed to the altars where offerings had been placed. She prayed, "The sisters' faces are rotten, and their bones buried. Take this offering and be pleased." Several months later, I learned that he was on the road to recovery.

I continued to follow this shaman and observed her extraordinary powers of intuition. Each patient's spiritual diagnosis was different. In each case, she reviewed the tragedies of their lives along with their entire medical histories. She often sent them back to the doctors to take their medicine and encouraged them to go to the hospital. Her most important contribution to the lives of these poor people was quite simple. She did what no doctor or health service could do: She restored the patients' will to live. With no way to improve their economic lives, she empowered them with ancestral spirits, created public support for their illness, and made a family's responsibility compliant with the doctor's orders. All that was possible because she

Mun Ok-Sun and me on her first visit to a Seoul department store

practiced her traditional healing arts in the homes and communities where the patients lived. She was one of them and understood their inner psychic, social, and economic burdens.

Like all religions, shamanism is a religion of affliction. Illness and spirituality have been inseparable throughout history from biblical healings of the blind to the Christian scientists and faith healers of modern times. However, it is peculiar to find the practice of shamanist religions side-by-side with modern medicine in developing nations. Such was the case on Jeju Island in the 1970s, and I was lucky to be its witness.

I never learned as much about healing as I did from this shaman. She was a warm and loving person who would serve anyone whether or not that person had the money to pay fees. There was a large spirit tree dedicated to the "agassi" (female) spirit in the middle of Jeju City. Her home was at that site because she felt close to the gods there. She was one of the last great traditional healers who only HAD disdain for the way in which Korean shamanism has become a tourist spectacle. She understood shamanism's principles as a religion with no temple, no bible, and no fixed priesthood. Today, its future is uncertain because without the great practitioners like Mun, it may retreat into the dark alleys of fortunetellers. Hidden from view, or gone forever, its songs and rituals may survive only as children's fairy tales.

Patricia Licuanan

My true heroes shun the limelight. Some leaders are willing to assume front positions but cleverly pass on credit for their achievements to everyone else. Dr. Patricia Licuanan is that kind of leader. In a crowded room, she stands out with her well-groomed Filipino style. She usually speaks with authority, as if in a lecture hall, but she never displays a condescending air.

Most of her Filipino colleagues know her as the efficient former president of Miriam College and a professor of psychology with a reputation for extraordinary scholarly work. She earned her doctoral degree in social psychology from Pennsylvania State University and a master's degree from Cornell University—both major achievements as she challenged the validity of Western theories during her student days. An expert on gender and economic policy, migrant women, adolescents and child-rearing practices, she also published outstanding work in conflict management and cross-cultural communications. Her research into psychology theory and extensive academic writings earned her the Psychological Association of the Philippines' Most Outstanding Psychologist award in 1988. An active applied social sci-

• Patricia Licuanan

entist, she nevertheless gets her greatest satisfaction from watching students blossom and achieve. She primarily sees herself as an educator.

However, anyone who has seen this professor at the UN knows that she is also an accomplished politician. As head of her government delegation and former chairperson of the Commission on the Status of Women from 1993 to 1995, Licuanan acted as a facilitator and arbiter in two major UN political blocs: the Asia Group and Task Force for the Group of 77. During the 1995 Beijing Women's Conference, she chaired the Main Committee, where the toughest issues were sent for resolution. I watched her smoothly navigate a roomful of disgruntled, sometimes hostile, delegates, many of whom viewed her as an inexperienced newcomer to the intrigues of international diplomacy. At the same time, she also had to harness discussions with rowdy NGOs and resolve tensions between feminists and fundamentalists. Something about her manner was always authoritative.

Her social psychology skills helped her untangle diplomatic knots and win support for controversial calls. Typically, she would crack a joke at the height of tensions or disarm the combatants with comments like "Hey guys, give me a break." If you want to get the crowds' attention in a huge UN hall, it doesn't hurt to be a regal woman with a winning smile.

She is affectionately called "tatti" and is one of a growing number of humanist-feminist leaders who are trying to improve human welfare by looking at the world through women's eyes. Like Wangari Maathai of Kenya and Ela Bhatt of India, she has an enduring commitment to making sure that gender equality is never forgotten and helping make miracles happen.

She is inspired in part by the Licuanan family tradition. Her great-grandfathers, both ardent nationalists, were members of the Filipino constitutional congress at the birth of the nation. Licuanan's grandmother was a university professor and one of the country's first women English language short story writers. Her mother wrote a daily column for *The Manila Chronicle*. With such pace-setting role models, it never occurred to the young Licuanan to be a traditional homemaker. After graduating from the Maryknoll High School, she went to the remote island of Mindanao to live and work with peasants.

"I was city born and bred and I never had much rural experience," she told me. "I was an idealist and wanted to serve my country and the poor."

When I first met her in 1977, she had taken a brief recess from her university career to work with UNICEF in Thailand. Her task was to help the organization define its first regional women's program. She did this with her usual high energy and drive. Once she set the program into motion, she felt compelled to return to the country that she loved so well. She would never work as a UN civil servant again. Nevertheless, at every opportunity over the next two decades, she opened doors for women's groups, NGOs, and her government to connect with regional and international projects.

After her UN days, Licuanan has continued to be a one-person support group for a myriad of organizations. As chair of the Filipino First project, she helped select 100 outstanding women leaders in the country's history. She sat on the Board of the Magsaysay Foundation that grants the prestigious Magsaysay award for service to humanity. The Bishop-Businessmen's Conference for Human Development, a coalition of Filipino businesses and church laity working for economic development, could count on her for valuable advice. Other research and training centers, such as the Gaston Z. Ortigas Peace Institute, sought her consultation on key policy decisions. Her schedule of international committee meetings included the ASEAN Committee on Social Development and UNESCO.

Licuanan admitted to me that she was obsessed with making sure the Beijing Women's Conference was not a waste of time.

"I must confess that I still have my Beijing hangover," she wrote. "But unlike with most hangovers, I am determined to nurse this one for as long as possible in myself, as well as in others, in order that the spirit of the Conference carry over into the difficult work of implementation."

In an era of growing political cynicism and moral uncertainty, women like Patricia Licuanan stand out as role models for others. Her unflinching optimism is reflected in her belief that personal transformation is possible for everyone, even her enemies. I admire most the purity of her ambitions. She is an exceptional achiever, but if she never wins recognition, she will still persevere in a lifetime of service.

The Owl

In 1900, my aunt was born in Pyongyang, Korea, ten years before Japanese colonial rule began. Her name was Song Pok-Shyn, which meant "blessing of faith," but her friends nicknamed her "the owl" for her big eyes and her love of staying up late. My grandfather, Song Sang-Chum, did not care for flowery feminine names, so he gave all of his daughters names with abstract, serious meanings like "unchanging faith," "respectful," and "straightforward morality." The care he took in naming his children was only the beginning of his lavish attention to their upbringing.

My grandfather was a powerful landlord and owner of an international textile business, and his ambition was to use his wealth to modernize Korea. Like the social reformers of his time who set up independence societies and spoke out for women's human rights, he was convinced that a colonial threat would become a reality if Korea did not catch up with the rest of the world and open its doors to international influence. He advocated for radical ideas, like the introduction of modern science and culture and especially the education of girls. He planned to send his children as "envoys" abroad to study foreign

• Korean delegates – Convention of the student volunteer movement, Detroit, Michigan (Dec. 1927 - Jan 1928)

society and then bring them home to carry out reforms.

There was one problem. In traditional Korean culture, only boys were educated and had careers. Since he had one son and four daughters, he had to make some hard decisions. Instead of taking a second wife in order to have male offspring (common for aristocrats in his day), he raised his daughters as if they were sons. According to my mother, he bragged that he wouldn't trade a single girl in exchange for a bunch of boys.

Driven by his dream, he was prepared to break all conventions. In an era when most upper-class daughters were secluded and quietly shuffled off into arranged marriages, he let his daughters play sports and be seen in public without the traditional skirted veil. Instead of leaving his inheritance to his eldest son, he divided the land, business, buildings, and other properties equally among his children.

He made similarly unorthodox decisions about his daughters' schooling. In Pyongyang, a handful of girls were allowed to attend

Dr. Song Pok-Shyn as a student

Christian schools, but no one sent them to college. However, to prepare them for higher education, my grandfather sent his daughters to mission schools, such as the Soongeui High School, to learn foreign languages. Then he sent all but his eldest daughter to study abroad in Japan and the United States. Each of his children specialized in a subject that he thought would help Korea's development in agriculture, medicine, and Western music. He decided that my aunt's task would be to run the first Korean-owned modern medical hospital, which he built during her college days. He named it "PoHwa" or "The Treasure of Peace" because he thought that the greatest gift of all was harmony between people.

However, he never found that treasure in his lifetime. The Japanese military takeover of Korea in 1910 confirmed his worst fears. The colonial policies turned quickly toward complete assimilation. Korean families had to take Japanese names, and Korean was declared a foreign language. Japan reorganized the public school system to favor Japanese colonists, took tight control over businesses and agriculture, and siphoned off the country's resources to fill Japan's coffers. As colonial rule became harsher, my grandfather became more and more resolved to resist it. However, the family paid a price.

My grandmother was the first member of the family to be arrested, presumably for helping to finance Korean independence through her Methodist TongAh women's group. My grandfather's political ideals for Korean independence affected my aunt as well. She proved to be even more militant than he was.

Dr. Song Pok-Shyn at Japan medical school with friend

Soon after she enrolled in the elite Tokyo Women's College of Medicine, my aunt befriended Rhee Seung-Man, Kim Do-Yeon, Chang Duk-Su, and other leaders of the underground Korean students' Independence Movement. Fluent in Japanese and able to travel freely between Tokyo and Seoul, she agreed to be a messenger, carrying information from Japan through Seoul for the provisional Korean government exiled in Manchuria. Women in the student movement were so rare that it took the Japanese secret police a number of months to discover her identity. They finally arrested her while she traveled on a train from Pusan to Seoul. She was 19 years old.

She was kept in solitary confinement for weeks in Seoul's Namsan prison, then brought out of her cell for interrogation. Decades later, before tucking me into bed, she would tell me stories of her revolutionary days. Each tale was woven into a moral and political lesson. My aunt didn't really mean to frighten me, but I lived and felt every word. My childish imagination even exaggerated her tales until her life became part of my dreams.

She said that in prison, she was brought out from the dark, half-blinded by the light, trembling. Then, she was hung upside-down by her feet and asked for names of her friends in the underground movement. When she refused to answer, the police filled her nose with water. She coughed up water, then blood. Her hands were black and blue from bamboo shreds pierced under the nails. My grandfather's physician friend came to the rescue and told Japanese authorities she would die soon in their hands if she were not released. They put her body on a funeral cot, pushed her outside the prison doors, and turned their attention to the living.

Later, the Japanese police informed my aunt that she must leave the country or return to prison. She told my grandfather that she would flee to the United States but could never return to Korea. He was heartbroken. My aunt left for the United States, became a Barbour Scholar at the University of Michigan, and graduated in 1929 as the first Korean to receive a PhD in Public Health. Always an independent thinker, she wrote her dissertation about vitamin C therapy, a very controversial subject at the time. Even her sense of how women should behave showed her contempt for convention. By Korean standards, she did outrageously modern things, like cut her hair short and marry an Anglo-American.

Her political life was also conducted in her own way with a personal power network and grand dinners. After graduation, she turned her attention to Washington, acting as an informal ambassador for the Korean provisional government. She befriended Eleanor Roosevelt, members of the Supreme Court, and US Army generals in an effort to influence American policy in Korea.

On March 1, 1941, a group of about 40 Koreans met in Washington for a Korean Liberty Congress at the Lafayette Hotel. Their purpose was to lobby against the possible American bombing of Korea. I looked closely at the photo taken on that occasion and noticed something odd. Most of the women, who were wives of the delegates, were

• Liberty congress in Washington DC (1942)

dressed in fashionable Western clothes. My aunt, who was standing next to the Korean president-to-be, Rhee Seung-Man, was wearing a traditional Korean dress. In any context, she had to be different from other women. This was her feminist trademark.

She had the advantage of having inherited women's equality as a family value. She didn't have to be shy in the company of men or step back and let them take the lead. My grandfather gave her the rare gift of parental approval and freedom to make her own political choices. He also made sure that she had the educational status that gave her the clout in Korean culture to make Korean men listen. Much like Helen Kim and Esther Park, the women leaders in Korea's first women's movement, my aunt knew that the stakes were high. Her generation counted many firsts for the country: the first women novelists, the first women politicians, the first women medical doctors. Many were so dedicated to breaking new ground that they never married or had children.

My aunt taught me many lessons that apply today. One lesson is that good causes make powerful enemies. In politics, you must always watch your back for enemies preparing to strike. Be most alert when they seem to be at rest. My aunt also showed me that cowardice and betrayal of one's conscience have no placc in a movement for liberation. They are fates worse than imprisonment. Growing up with such values made my life so much easier to steer. More than ever, I realize that family stories are the best legacy I can give to future generations.

My aunt had a love for her country, a love much like the love of a child for her mother or a woman for her lover. She was afraid that someday, a powerful nation would again threaten Korea's independence. Even though we lived in the United States, her young descendants were her only weapons to help safeguard Korea's future.

"You will always be a Korean," she said. "Americans will judge Korea by what you say and do. That is why you must try to be the best and help your country."

Separated from Korea by a vast ocean, she invented ways to keep the country close to her. Her nieces and nephews became its unofficial citizens and she, their queen mother. I have never known a woman who lived for her nation more than she did. When she died in California at the age of 94, she whispered her mother's name and hummed a melody in her last breath. My mother, who was at her side, said that it was the Korean national anthem.

Alda Facio

Gender justice needs its champions, and lawyers like Alda Facio are among the best. At any moment, she could cast a broad smile that is so appealing, it could win a case, even in the absence of a legal argument. Costa Rican judge, Alda Facio, once presided over the troubles of a broken civil society. Laborers with grievances and women seeking alimony stood before her, awaiting her calm and decisive judgment. She could have climbed the hierarchy to become a privileged member of the legal elite. Instead, she jumped down off the bench to stand with the women's movement. She wanted her political perspectives to be in touch with reality from the bottom up.

In the 1990s, she had a dual role. As director of the Women, Gender and Justice Program at the Latin American UN Institute for Crime Prevention, she oversaw research and training activities. Her program designed a methodology to help women lawyers and judges interpret the UN Convention on the Elimination of All Forms of Discrimination against Women.

Then, her work became more directly political. Throughout the final treaty conference on the International Criminal Court (ICC),

• Alda Facio

she coordinated the lobbying efforts of the Women's Caucus for Gender Justice in the ICC. Like a police officer on an emergency call, Facio responded to the situation at hand. She helped bring together consensus while adhering to a principle of wide consultation among the hundreds of women's groups represented.

There were many points on the caucus's agenda that Facio held dear. The protection of witnesses and victims and ensuring gender awareness among judges and officers appointed to ICC positions were two of her most important points. She also hoped that a political precedent was being established.

"It is a historic moment," Facio said. "For the first time in the history of the UN, women's groups were helping to shape an international institution of great magnitude from its beginnings." A major accomplishment of the Caucus was the addition of rape as a war crime in the draft ICC document.

Facio's evolution as a feminist activist was rooted in the history of her native Costa Rica. Her childhood home was abuzz with late-night meetings of the Democratic Socialist Party that her father helped to establish. The family conversations revolved around the future of an entire nation and how to create a nonviolent democracy.

Then came a rude awakening. As a college student in the 1960s in

Montgomery, Alabama, she learned how it felt to come from the opposite side of the tracks. She was the only Latin American citizen on campus. On her first day at school, the dean of the college told her that they had a problem; her passport said that she was Caucasian, and she was not. According to the school administration, being Latin American meant that she was colored. Taken aback by this novel experience with racial discrimination, Facio readily agreed to be recorded as a black student. The consequences were serious.

"The dean told the whole school I wasn't white, so I had to eat by myself," she said. Then, an African-American male student was admitted. The administrators got more confused and told her that she could not eat with him because she looked white. The two disregarded the rules, and then Ku Klux Klan members took matters into their own hands. They beat the young man up, broke his teeth, and landed him in the hospital. Facio's father, then-ambassador from Costa Rica to the United States, came to the rescue, and she resumed a normal student life in Rhode Island.

She told me that she never forgot how it felt to be a victim of racism. Her legal studies gave her the tools to analyze and speak on behalf of the oppressed. Putting a difficult marriage behind her, she discovered her feminist consciousness and began to reshape law through women's eyes. She founded one of Latin America's first feminist magazines, *Ventana* (Window), and helped establish CIMA, a network of international non-governmental organizations working on human rights issues. She then designed programs to investigate the conditions of women in prisons and psychiatric hospitals and to train judges and police. Facio is an international defender for the rights of thousands of women she will never meet.

Charlotte Bunch

When Charlotte Bunch talks about feminist politics, we all listen. She isn't a shouter; on the contrary, she speaks in a steady, careful tone, as if she is measuring the impact of each word. She particularly cares about how her opinions affect others.

According to Gloria Steinem, Bunch is a touchstone of the women's movement. Steinem often said, "Sooner or later—and on any hard questions of feminist theories of tactics comes—one is likely to hear: 'But what does Charlotte think?'" Inducted into the American National Women's Hall of Fame, Bunch is best known for her leadership in putting the concept of "women's rights as human rights" onto the agenda of the 1993 Human Rights conference in Vienna.

The founder and former executive director of the Center for Women's Global Leadership at Rutgers University, she has been an activist, author, and organizer in the women's and civil rights movements for more than 40 years. She was also founding director of the Public Resources Center, a fellow at the Institute for Policy Studies, and founder of the feminist publication, Quest. What I like most about her is that she never takes these titles as seriously as she does the

• Charlotte Bunch

ideas behind them.

There are two outstanding characteristics of Bunch's approach to politics. First, she is a peacemaker who looks for common ground in the midst of diversity. She even agrees with the Holy See on issues of poverty. She attributes her peacemaker approach partly to her family origins.

"I grew up in Artesia, a small conservative town in New Mexico," she explained. Her parents were Methodist would-be missionaries whose ambitions to work in China were thwarted by the Second World War. "They changed course and decided to work among America's rural poor," Bunch says. "I didn't grow up thinking [that] I was in the center of the universe."

She believes that "good" feminism affirms differences by race, sexual orientation, abilities, cultures, and religion. In her view, American feminists have to be willing to meet women from other countries on a more equal footing.

Charlotte Bunch, Noeleen Heyzer, Roxanna Corillo and Peggy Antropus (1995)

"Politically, I work as an American engaged most of my life in trying to change the US as well," Bunch said. "During the Human Rights Conference in Vienna, we decided to present the problems of violence against women domestically in the US so that people wouldn't think that violence is a product only of dictatorships and war."

A second characteristic of Bunch's politics is continual evolution: personal and political. She has trekked the rocky road from a naive campaigner for justice within the Christian student movement to socialist feminism, radical separatism, and international activism. Her early days looked very different from her today. In the 1960s, she worked mostly through the church, the YMCA, and the Methodist student's organizations as the founding president of the University Christian movement. She soon became involved in the civil rights movement during which she confronted the blatant racism of the South and saw a world through a new prism that affected the rest of her life.

In 1966, she graduated with a degree in history and political science. Professor Ann Scott advised her to "settle down and stop [her] activism." When Bunch asked if she couldn't both get a degree and work in activism, Bunch responded, "OK, I'm not going to graduate school."

Not all of her life decisions were so certain.

"I've had many crises of faith," she said. "When I became a feminist and when I came out as a lesbian, I felt that the church couldn't handle it, and I couldn't handle it not handling it. You have to continually re-evaluate the political perspective you work from because the work keeps changing." As she wrote in her book, *Passionate Politics*, she even experienced a mid-life crisis as a movement organizer, occasionally wishing that she had become a lawyer or a bookkeeper or something financially stable and accepted.

She hung on, and today, she is acclaimed as an historic leader in the women's human rights movement. She admits to getting discouraged and angry, but she can't see anything else she would rather be doing.

"I have learned over the years to have an openness. Life is unpredictable, and you stay engaged, open to the idea that something different happens," she said. Her priorities include highlighting issues of discrimination in education, legal, economic, and political rights. She is particularly concerned about violence against women, which she believes is the weapon by which patriarchy regenerates its authority.

When weary from campaigning, Bunch seems to find within herself an energy that sometimes pushes the limits of common sense. Her battle against breast cancer was a sober reminder to slow down. Nevertheless, Bunch is, above all, a pilgrim in search of the root causes of injustice. On her life journey, she seems to check under each stone for a wrong decision that doesn't measure up to her own high standards of truth and humility.

Alphabet Soup

ASG – Assistant Secretary General
BPfA – Beijing Platform for Action
CEDAW – Convention on the Elimination of All Forms of Discrimination against Women
CSW – Commission on the Status of Women
DESA – United Nations Department of Economic and Social Affairs
ECA – Economic Commission for Africa
ESCAP – Economic and Social Commission for Asia and the Pacific
ECE – Economic Commission for Europe
ECLAC – Economic Commission for Latin America & the Caribbean
ECOSOC – UN Economic and Social Council
ESCWA – Economic and Social Commission for West Asia
GA – General Assembly
ICPD – International Conference on Population & Development
IDP – Internally Displaced Person
ILO – International Labour Organization
IMF – International Monetary Fund
LAC – Latin America & the Caribbean
NGO – Non-Governmental Organization
OHCHR – Office of the High Commissioner of Human Rights
SDG – Sustainable Development Goals
UNAIDS – Joint United Nations Programme on HIV/AIDS
UNDP – UN Development Program
UNEP – UN Environment Program

UNESCO – UN Educational, Scientific & Cultural Organization
UNFCCC – UN Framework Convention on Climate Change
UNHCR – UN High Commissioner for Refugees
UNICEF – United Nation International Emergency Children's Fund
UNFPA – United Nations Population Fund
UNWomen – UN Entity for Gender Equality and the Empowerment of Women
WHO – World Health Organization

Online Resources

Beijing Platform for Action
http://www.un.org/womenwatch/daw/beijing/platform/

Commission on the Status of Women
https://www.unwomen.org/en/csw

Convention on the rights of the Child
http://www.unicef.org/crc/

Convention on the Elimination of All Forms of Discrimination against Women
http://www.un.org/womenwatch/daw/cedaw/

Food and Agriculture Organization
http://www.fao.org/home/en/

High Level Political Forum on Sustainable Development
https://sustainabledevelopment.un.org/hlpf

ILO conventions
http://www.ilo.org/global/standards/lang--en/index.htm

Rio Earth Summit
http://sustainabledevelopment.un.org/content/documents/Agenda21.pdf

World Summit for Social Development
http://www.un.org/esa/socdev/wssd/text-version/

Sustainable Development Goals
https://sdgs.un.org/#goal_section

UN Fourth World Conference on Women
https://www.unwomen.org/en/how-we-work/intergovernmental-support/world-conferences-on-women

UN Women
https://www.unwomen.org/en

World Conference on Human Rights
http://www.ohchr.org/EN/ABOUTUS/Pages/ViennaWC.aspx